DARKNESS BEFORE THE DAWN

BETWEEN THE TESTAMENTS

James E. Kifer

New Harbor Press
RAPID CITY, SD

Copyright © 2022 by James E. Kifer.

All rights reserved. No part of this publication may be reproduced, distributed or transmitted in any form or by any means, including photocopying, recording, or other electronic or mechanical methods, without the prior written permission of the publisher, except in the case of brief quotations embodied in critical reviews and certain other noncommercial uses permitted by copyright law. For permission requests, write to the publisher, addressed "Attention: Permissions Coordinator," at the address below.

Kifer/New Harbor Press
1601 Mt. Rushmore Rd., Ste 3288
Rapid City, SD 57701
www.NewHarborPress.com

Ordering Information:
Quantity sales. Special discounts are available on quantity purchases by corporations, associations, and others. For details, contact the "Special Sales Department" at the address above.

Darkness Before the Dawn / James E. Kifer. -- 1st ed.
ISBN 978-1-63357-436-6

Contents

PREFACE 1
CHAPTER ONE – RETURN FROM EXILE 13
CHAPTER TWO – THE UNSTOPPABLE PERSIAN TIDE 27
CHAPTER THREE – THE GLORY THAT WAS GREECE 39
CHAPTER FOUR – GOD'S GREAT SERVANTS 51
CHAPTER FIVE – TO THE STRONGEST 71
CHAPTER SIX – THE DESTROYER OF GOD 83
CHAPTER SEVEN – THE RETURN OF JOSHUA
AND DAVID 97
CHAPTER EIGHT – THE GRANDEUR
THAT WAS ROME 111
CHAPTER NINE – WARS AND RUMORS OF WARS 125
CHAPTER TEN – CROSSING THE RUBICON 137
CHAPTER ELEVEN – PEACE IN ROME:
WAR IN JUDEA 149
CHAPTER TWELVE – DESCENT INTO DIVISION 163
CHAPTER THIRTEEN - EPIPHANY 183
CHAPTER FOURTEEN – THE PREPARATION
OF THE CANVAS 197

PREFACE

The author recalls a day long ago when he was in the seventh grade at Ada Junior High School in Ada, Oklahoma, and was a student in an art class taught by Miss Hargis. Her skills as an art teacher were far beyond those of the twelve-year-old who was nevertheless making a reasonably diligent effort to do his best in a subject in which he had but little natural ability. One afternoon Miss Hargis placed before the class a copy of a painting to demonstrate a lesson in perspective, proportionality, and emphasis. The painting was quite "busy" and depicted a scene in an early American colonial port. In the foreground on the left side was a group of persons clad in somewhat austere black and white colonial garb, and they were the most prominent figures in the scene. Their gaze was not upon each other but upon some object in the distance. It was a scene in broad daylight, with many dockworkers rolling barrels, preparing various cargoes to be placed in the ships that were docked in the port. Other persons were busy with various tasks in the foreground. The port waters itself displayed large two and three masted ships with sailors, and officers aboard loading and unloading cargoes, great and small. As noted, it was a very busy scene, but nothing about any of these persons or activities really engaged the person's eye beyond the momentary. The artist, whether unknown or forgotten by the author, had so designed this work that the observer's attention was drawn to the ocean's horizon in the upper right-hand corner of the painting. There, a small object, but upon examination definitely a sailing ship, was quietly heading into port. The skills of the artist and the perspective and setting of those persons on the dock immediately riveted attention to the ship, still little more than a miniaturized toy image, in the distance. Yet, the attentive observer, even a twelve-year-old, knew that the center of the painting's attention was not the larger objects and persons in the foreground, but rather the ship, herein portrayed as insignificant in size, coming into port.

Not just in artistry, though, is the apparently small, even seemingly insignificant, engulfed by the larger proportioned objects, the so-called "big picture" which is more flamboyant, colorful, noisy, and even temporarily, at least, more interesting. When the panoply of history is spread before us the inconspicuous is most often missed, overlooked, or even purposely ignored. So, it is even with the most important events in not just the world's history but in the story of all Creation itself. The Old Testament is a compilation of thirty-nine books from Genesis through Malachi. The story of creation, the fall of man, the designation of the Hebrews as God's Chosen People and their history is told, often in spectacular style and intricate detail. Yet, the Book really trails off with the last words being from the prophet Malachi in circa 400 B.C., a prophet who despaired of the state of God's Chosen. Nothing more is written of those people, the Israelites until their story, soon to be subsumed in a greater narrative begins anew with the gospel writers, commencing with Matthew, approximately four centuries later. The scriptures are silent, but the world kept turning around. In fact, the next four hundred years have supplied enough fascinating personalities, new, innovative ideas, cultural works, and progress that the era and its personalities are intensively studied yet today. Briefly we will extend our observations to briefly conscript for study the hundred years which backward commencing about 500 B.C., so that some of the most seminal events in all history may be noted. In this half millennium the very foundations of Western Civilization were not only lain but were built upon with astonishing success. This is the time replete with names ever famous, royal, and political luminaries of the historical glory and glamour of Alexander the Great, Julius Caesar, Augustus Caesar, Antony and Cleopatra, Xerxes, and Hannibal ad infinitum. It was a time that began to explode but explode generally (but not always) in luminous beauty, the beauty of ideas, of beautiful art, magnificent structure, and even representative government. Peoples and nations, which in the Old Testament are glancingly mentioned, in the background or are absent entirely come to the fore, primarily the Persians, but especially the Greeks and the Romans. Notwithstanding their importance to the work and its theme, none of these will be the subject of any real historical study.

Customarily a preface sets forth the author's reasons for the book, the outline, scope, and depth of what is to follow and its general raison d'tre. In so doing a brief outline of the work and its schematic theme will ensue, and these efforts intentions are to provide such. Before, though, a definition and summary of the work, its line of logic and reason, all of which are given in hope of giving the reader a tentative taste of the substance which follows. We intend not to be remiss in this matter, but before offering a preview of the book's contents and premises it is our compulsion to explain and delineate the negative, i.e., what the book "is not." Actually, this small work is not many things. By no recognizable definition is this intended to be a history of any people, any civilization, or a biography of any person.

The history of the period from 500 B.C. to the dawn of a new dispensation is beyond replete with historical works devoted to its studies. Some are contemporaneous with the events they describe and are effectively cornerstones of Western historical writing. Greeks such as Herodotus and Thucydides and Roman writers of the calibre of Livy and Tacitus are still studied with intensity. In the two millennia hence other classics, most notably Edward Gibbons <u>The Decline and Fall of the Roman Empire</u> are themselves, even while borne out of due season, classical works. Modern contemporary historians have produced from their ranks excellent ancient historians who have continually illuminated a fascinating historical epoch, and they tell in intricate and fascinating detail the colorful stories of men and women, their characters and personalities, their romances, the battles they fought, the nations and even empires which they forged and ruled. These five hundred years maintain a shining historical patina to modern and post-modern societies today, and in some regards appear in no danger of having the glitter of their historical luster dim. The serious historian and the historical buff both continually find their anticipation and hopes rewarded with each year's production of new histories of storied ancient realms, Persia, Greece and Rome and biographies of the ever-fascinating Alexander, the Persian rulers, and the Roman Caesars.

Yet, really, does it remain for any "new history" to be produced? Have not the stories been told and refashioned and then told again and the sometimes scarce historical sources been so thoroughly examined that nothing new is to be found? Certainly, good books and articles written by good, even historically eminent, and outstanding authors will continue to be produced, but the story itself was over some two thousand years ago.

Still, only rarely and glancingly has a central question ever been asked, much less its having, received a detailed expository answer. What did it all mean? Yes, it has been taught for centuries, these stories of how our Western civilization was lain and arose primarily through the brilliant intellectual prowess of the Greeks and the organizational genius and determination of the Romans. The development of arts and engineering, towns, cities, buildings practical governmental structures have certainly been discussed, at times brilliantly. So, too, the bloodletting replete in battles and wars, the coupling and uncoupling of the "great" has always provoked interest and commentary and has retained a lurid charm which shows no signs of abatement. Yet, what did it all mean spiritually and for the sake of eternity? Did the God of the Bible, the God of the Hebrews, a deity unmentioned by the Greeks and Romans have any influence in it all? Were these five hundred years simply a procession of random events or was there an invisible or unseen linkage moving ever so slowly forward according to a Divine Plan? Metaphorically did that tiny sailing vessel on the horizon ignored by almost all, ever develop into something of vast dominant importance? To momentarily complete the metaphorical inquiry, we seek to answer that question (of course, yes) and describe how it became not just the center of that artistic scene but the center of the universe itself.

This is a history per se of no one, and for reasons heretofore given. It will, though, employ an historical structure of well-known events and persons and briefly retell their stories. Chronologically it begins circa 500 B.C. in the Empire of the Persian King Darius, a sprawling conglomeration of nations, states, kingdoms and the like greater than the world had ever seen. The story of Darius and his son Ahasuerus (a/k/a Xerxes) and their insatiable appetites for even more, gargantuan desires that culminated in two wars and four of history's most famous battles against pitifully outnumbered foes from the poor, rocky land called Greece. In point of time, they are first, but our narrative naturally opens with the people who God had declared His Chosen, reduced in might and power to essentially nothing and in numbers to a remnant only. The first chapter will examine their condition as seen through the observing lens of a man named Malachi, the last of the Old Testament prophets. Yet this is certainly not to be a history of the Jews "between the Testaments." Then over two centuries of the Jews' history will be omitted, and barely a mention of this people will be made again until Chapter Six.

Chapters Three through Five bring to center stage those two cultures mentioned together so frequently that they mesh in the minds of many as one, Greece and Rome. Still, though, western history and culture have long denominated them as "classical civilization" they were two (perhaps even more) distinct entities that while influencing each other, their points of divide may still be boldly drawn. It is in this section of the book that the rise of one of history's giant personages is made, neither from Greece nor Rome but from a realm on its northern border that the Greeks conceded a recognition of only partial civilization. He was an astonishingly young man, King of Macedonia at age twenty and forever known as Alexander the Great. His rise and influence will be accounted incalculably important and great. The son of one of ancient history's most famous and successful rulers, King Philip II of Macedonia, Alexander will be seen as one who welded his native Macedonia together with Greece and achieved conquests with an apparently invincible army that he had forged. Few scholars, few historians, will deny Alexander's place in the sun, but was he just one of the most successful of the world's conquerors or did his incredibly brief life have a far greater effect and meaning?

In the wake of Alexander's conquests and legacy we will note their effect, nor merely the temporal effects of battles, national boundaries, kings, queens, princes, and princesses but the indelible imprimatur which Alexander's life left on culture, language, and religion, even to the juncture where Alexander's unslakeable thirst for conquest perhaps was co-opted by a Divine plan for something far greater.

In Chapter Seven our gaze will again refocus upon God's Chosen, the Jews, and for the first time in literally thousands of years we must do so without benefit of scriptural history. The Jews' history was told in the Old Testament, but their lives, like anyone anytime, were lived day by sometimes monotonous and usually unremarkable day. This small nation was never an ancient power, and though its people were no longer slaves they were inevitably living under foreign, which to the Jews always meant, alien and unlawful authority. As the timelines move and the spotlights of history ever refocus their beams on the new the Jewish state becomes somewhat of a backwater until the rise of a savage Greco-Syrian ruler who sought to literally destroy this people in a precursor to the more infamous Holocaust of the twentieth century. Here the fantasy of a twin historical sage is exposed and exploded. The ill described "secular" history of kings and other potentates' clashes with a savagery and the heroism of a family of five brothers who step forward to save the Jewish nation and their strange devotion to only one God. They are successful, and much of the structure for what follows in the New Testament almost two centuries hence is here lain.

No people, no nation, no culture and neither man nor woman develops in an isolated channel, fully walled off from the world's developments. In the full spectrum of its grandeur the truth of this assertion will be seen when this tiny nation of Judah survives its first holocaust only to begin to come within the orbit and eventually the sovereignty of the great power from the west, the mightiest the world had ever witnessed, Rome.

Rome, first in its republican for and later in its manifestation as an empire gradually consumes the earth and all its kingdoms. It becomes the arena in which the main events of the day are played, to sometimes shocking and invariably bloody, even gory, conclusions. The New Testament world, awaiting just beyond the horizon of history, will be in the main a Roman world. Yet before we touch upon the Biblical records once again some titanic events and not just larger than life but larger than history personalities will be examined. These are men and women, both scholastically and popularly, whose stars of enticing interest have yet to dim, even into the self-styled and self-congratulatory post-modern twenty-first century. Figures which yet today radiate on historical glory such Julius Caesar were Roman, but their influence in Biblical events was profound and lasting.

Finally, our brief narrative, this centuries long story of kings, generals, armies, battles, wars, and rumors of wars will culminate quietly in not just an obscure, but really an unknown, village in the Judean province of Galilee, a backwater sector of a small and despised Roman province. There a messenger from God will appear to an unknown teenage girl and deliver the most important message this world of noisy clash and clamor has ever heard.

Now we pause to acknowledge that the interested reader is fully entitled to pose a question. If this be not a history, then exactly what is offered, for its outline sounds quite like a standard history. Further, the inquiry may be made as to how and why any of this has to do with a story which begins with a Jewish return from exile and closes with an angelic prophecy to a "nobody." Still, this remains not a history, for we readily admit that the history has been told often and told well. Our musings merely poach upon the extant records and attempt (hopefully with at least a modicum of success) to tie together seemingly unrelated events spread over a five-hundred-year span and a huge geographical expanse. To the reader with an historical interest the stories remain fascinating, but were they, as is the common modern conceit, unrelated happenings by persons separated by time and geography who knew each other not at all? Was this half millennium of history just another sunspot on the evolutionary timeline of happenstance, or was there in the present modern phrase an "intelligent design" in back of it all, a master historical artist fashioning the affairs of men for His own purposes? We opt for the latter, and it is to this end that the subjects, stories, and players should be understood.

In scriptural terms the ways of God are different than those of humanity, and so are the means and persons He employs to fashion His designs. In constructing this particular (and quite likely, peculiar) saga of events three general topics will command out attention. The first, as in any story of this earth, is the participants, those people who by their wills, positions, powers, and proclivities set the pace and drive forward the ideas and events. A precautionary warning is here mandatory. Most, but not all, these individuals, in the plainest of terms are bad, evil, wicked, devilish, self-willed, and even almost Satanic, yet their lives moved forward the historical vessel to harbor.

Our contention is that God utilizes the bad as well as the good for the working and accomplishment of His purposes. The believing Christian is not from the inception of his or her faith that both Testaments are resplendent with men and women of heroic proportions, persons who possessed the character and commitment of Noah, Abraham, Joseph, Elijah, Isaiah, Jeremiah, all the apostles, Mary, the sisters Mary and Martha, and an endless array of shining lights. Easily we see that the God of Creation, the God of the Universe worked His will and His way through persons such as this. But did He not utilize as well the darker side of human behavior, seen in the avariciousness, cruelty, and unbounded ambition of men of the fame and moral caliber of King Xerxes of the Persians, the brutal soldiery of Sparta, Alexander the Great, Julius Caesar and his nephew Octavian? A central thesis of this work is that God employed (and still employs) whomever He wishes or desires to further His will. Coupled with this assertion, the flip side of the coin if you will, is the strong and substantial belief that especially if God is in the equation, there are no such elements as happenstance, luck, or coincidence. In God's eternal but here terrestrial drama, to borrow from William Shakespeare, "All the world's a stage, and all the men and women merely players." Most of the men this preface has referenced by name neither ever heard of the God of the Bible or if they did, He was brushed away as not worthy of their thoughts and musings. Their minds and their actions were often on war, conquest, self-aggrandizement and with many, self-glorification. As we referenced, these were not admirable persons. Interesting, yes, and to many fascinating, but certainly not worthy of admiration or emulation.

The God of the Universe, as offered by the One who knew Him best, is explained as a God who has numbered the hairs on the head of every person who has ever been animate and notices when a mere sparrow, supposedly of no consequence, falls to earth. Such a God's presence and influence must be noted in ancient lands and cultures other than and in addition to His own Chosen, the Jews. This is not to state the God approved the brutal and vicious conquests of Alexander and Caesar, or even the wisdom, true and not-so-true, of the Greek philosophers, for God never sanctioned evil. The spreading of the ancient historical epic, this "between the testaments" story, though, demonstrates that He bent and shaped men, women, and events to His greater purpose.

When the Persian multitudes were twice held at bay at Thermopylae's pass by the legendary Spartan 300 and later soundly defeated by the Athenians God was present. A century and a half hence we will view history's most famous conquering general, Alexander the Great, as he more than returns the favor and exacts revenge over the Persians. He will be seen as a man of almost preternatural ability, lasting charisma and enough pride and ambition for an army. So, did the God of Creation work through this man as well?

It will not be all wars, battles, and bloodshed, though. In fact, those matters, as integral as they are to the story, are actually secondary. The dissemination of ideas, knowledge, culture and ultimately peace will be recognized as more important in this narrative.

As the conclusion to this perhaps too lengthy Preface is reached the author has two personal remarks to offer, whereupon he hopes that this book is bereft of further personal references. First, the author is neither a historian nor a theologian, yet he retains an abiding lifetime interest in each discipline. The historical facts and representations made herein have long been the historical consensus. The Biblical references and accounts of events are taken from the scriptures themselves. Except where scriptures themselves are quoted the author makes no representation of the absolute certainty of his offerings. In fact, the conclusions of myself or anyone else likely will contain some error, for the Mind of God is not fully understandable by us. Finally, we hearken once again to the painting, the recounting of which begins this work. The dockside activities and the busy persons will be the focus of our work until its final chapter, when the distant sailing ship finally arrives in harbor.

CHAPTER ONE – RETURN FROM EXILE

The patience of God, greater than anything even His most ardent and devoted disciples can imagine and far greater in scope and depth than the non-believer can ever demonstrate, eventually ran out. Always weak spiritually and more often than not openly contemptuous of God the northern kingdom of Israel gasped its last breaths in 722 B.C. when the dreaded Assyrians came from the north. Enslaving who they did not slaughter on the spot the Assyrian conquerors strung together like fish on a stringer, hooked in their mouths and lips, and dragged away most of God's Chosen People into slavery and ultimately oblivion. Israel, composed of ten of the original twelve tribes, as a distinct entity ceased existence. Gradually, over the years, the generations, and the centuries they inter-married among the Gentiles and lost their singularity of character as Jews. A few, those who had escaped forced emigration and slavery remained in portions of the old homeland of Israel, and they too intermingled with the Gentiles, eventually becoming known as the Samaritans, a people of great consequence Biblically and historically.

Only Judah in the south remained. Always more attentive to God than was its northern brother Israel, still Judah's history showed as much apostasy as loyalty. Its last great king, Josiah perished in battle in 609 B.C. Gradually, Judah succumbed to eastern invaders itself, and in 597 B.C. Jerusalem fell to the Babylonians under the famed King

Nebuchadnezzar, and the Jews were departed en masse, albeit by stages, to the east and became captive first to the Babylonians and later the Persians in 539 B.C., a still greater power whose giant polyglot empire had subsumed the Babylonians.

To borrow from a phrase that had yet to be coined, though, the conquest of Judah was a cloud with a silver lining. The Babylonians and then the Persians were definitely the rulers of the Jews, and as our account will later reflect, an incredibly diverse plethora of other nations. While the Jews had their masters and especially with the expenditure of time the Jews, while shorn of their national independence, retained considerable freedom and generally (although noteworthy exceptions will surface) had the freedom to practice their religion and worship God. Of great consequence in exile Judah began to develop men and women of exemplary character, a lineage which had seemingly faded away and expired in the pre-exilic days. Men, who while still in their youth, stepped forward with honor, dignity, and remarkable courage. Their names, such as Daniel, Shadrach, Meshach, and Abednego are as bright as any in the Bible. Later, Mordecai rose to high position in Persia, and his niece Esther presented a rare example of an extraordinary blending of beauty, wisdom, leadership, and courage. So, outstanding moral leadership was gradually returning to the Jewish people, yet each of those noted went the way of all flesh and left the scene. Eventually, with the Babylonians defeated only the Persians remained as subjugators of the Judean exiles, but this is an "only" of mammoth proportions. In the vastness of the Persian sovereignty the Jewish people were numerically and politically insignificant. As did the Assyrians with the people of Israel the Persians easily could have crushed the Jews, but they were too wise for that drastic horror. In many matters the Persians, of all the conquering nations of both the Old and New Testaments were the wisest and the least constraining in their rule. Perhaps the greatest and most famous of the Jewish exiles, the prophet and ruler Daniel, in his eponymous book prophesied the Persians as the second of the four great ancient empires. To our story and study the great attribute of the Persians that unite the other conquerors of the Jews, past and future, the Persian rulers willingly, albeit gradually emancipated the captive Jews and allowed them to return to Judah.

The Jewish return to their homeland, like all good things came from God, but the Creator utilized and moved through the men and women He chose (and does yet today) to accomplish His ends. Sometimes, those persons themselves are not even His followers and not necessarily fully admirable. The Babylonians had taken Jerusalem in 597 B.C. and under their great King Nebuchadnezzar had pilfered from the Temple all sorts of holy vessels, valuable in themselves and priceless to observant Jews. He was an erratic figure, arrogant, even hubristic but as an official he had a certain respect for the Jews, their religion and especially four young Jews who began to serve him, Daniel, Shadrach, Meshach, and Abednego. Babylon was the great power in this corner of the world, but its dominance was fleeting. Nebuchadnezzar's son and successor was Belshazzar. The Old Testament clearly marks Belshazzar as a profligate man and a libertine whose Babylonian Empire fell to the Persians in 539 B.C. The Persians were ruled and truly well led by one of the greatest and most accomplished leaders of antiquity, King Cyrus II. His reign was generally constructive, and he was masterful in conquest but more so in his ability to form alliances with other nations, especially the Medes, a people to the west of Persia and quite similar to the Persians themselves. To the historian this is all of interest, perhaps even of fascination, but for our narrative Cyrus II becomes important because he was the man selected by God to begin the fulfillment of a promise He had tendered to the prophet Jeremiah:

> "For thus saith the Lord,
> That after seventy years be accomplished at Babylon

> I will visit you, and perform by good word toward you,
> in causing you to return to this place."

God now had on the Persian throne perhaps its wisest occupant, and He determined that now that the seven decades of captivity had elapsed it was time for the Jews to return to Judah. They were not going, however, upon their own instigation and authority. Cyrus II ruled Persia still, but Cyrus, no Jew, became an integral part of the return from captivity when:

> "(T)he word of the Lord stirred up the spirit of Cyrus King of Persia,
> that he made a proclamation throughout all his kingdom,
> and put it also in writing, saying:
>
> Thus saith Cyrus, King of Persia, The Lord God of heaven,
> hath given me all the kingdom of the earth,
> and He hath charged me to build Him a house in Jerusalem,
> which is in Judah."

Likely the great king Cyrus knew quite little of the God of the Jews, his own captives. Yet, that God knew him, and just as He employed Pharaoh at the time of Moses and Nebuchadnezzar just a generation or two before to enact His will so now was Cyrus to be His servant. The distinction, though, is that Cyrus was aware of His being a servant. With the might, power and character of King Cyrus fully harnessed to God's will, it is an appropriate moment to recognize that God has always and still today uses who He wants, when He wants, how He wants and what He wants to His discretion. His power, in this and all regards, is without limitation.

The return from exile, though, would be no Hollywood-like cinematic spectacle of unlimited multitudes being led from bondage while inspirationally dramatic music arose in the background. More prosaically, this exodus to Judah was over an expanse of time, and many contingents of Jews were led by various leaders. Literally over the span of decades groups of Jews returned to their ancient homeland, and their sojourns were led by men with strange names, men such as Sheshbazzar and Zerubbabel, and likely others whose names are unknown. Most importantly, though, the Jews were back in Judah. Generations had elapsed since the Babylonians had uprooted them mercilessly and had carted them to strange foreign lands. Obviously, all the original exiles were deceased, but were their descendants who returned mere copies of their forebears?

THE REMNANT

Modern carpeting is manufactured, processed, and distributed by the roll. What comes from the carpet mill is "brand new," with a special feel and aroma, and depending on the tastes of the individual it may be spectacularly beautiful when unrolled and ultimately laid. The rooms in which carpets are placed, though, are seldom of proportions matching that of the carpet roll. The layers are forced to cut and trim the carpet to fit the dimensions of the room. What remains on the roll is called the remnant. The remnant is but a small piece of the large roll, still the same material, though, but lacking in the size and impressiveness of the roll from which it was taken. This piece of carpeting is made of precisely the same material as was the original product, but now it has been separated, literally cut, and torn from its original roll. Even before its being placed on the floor it has a bedazzled, perhaps even a worn, look from being handled roughly and often. Still, though, its original elemental integrity and beauty had faded, maybe even vanished, it still retains a utilitarian purpose. The God of the Jews, the God of the Bible, was certainly not reluctant in employing the concept and the very word "remnant." This is the perfect description of the small population of Jews who returned from seven decades of exile:

"And now for a little space grace hath been shown from the Lord our God,
to leave us a remnant to escape,
and to give us a nail in His holy place,
that our God may lighten our eyes,
and give us a little reviewing in our bondage."

This was Judah, and this so well describes the Jews, perhaps no more than 50,000 who returned from Babylonian and Persian captivity to begin again in their ancient homeland. These descendants of the slaves who Moses led from Egypt so very long ago were well treated by the mercy of God, as recognized by one of their greatest prophets, Isaiah:

"Except the Lord of hosts had left unto us a very small remnant,
we should have been as Sodom,
and we should have been like unto Gomorrah."

A remnant is not as beautiful as the original, is not as pleasingly proportioned, but it still serves a purpose. In fact, it is invaluable to the builder's structure and design, and it is necessary to the foundation's covering. So were the Jews who returned, but who were they? It is easy and a bit cynical to assume that these "latter day Jews" of the 500's and 400's B.C. were close replicas of their ancestors, but such a presumption requires evidence more than supposition and presumption.

Most importantly a distinction between past and present must be recognized almost to the point of overemphasis. The Jews had at last abandoned pagan idolatry. After witnessing the destruction of the northern kingdom of Israel and the near disappearance of Judah the Jews had turned from Baal and his many cohorts. At times their worship would range from tepid to nonexistent, God's laws would be twisted, distorted, and perverted, but it was the one true God, not heathen idols, before whom the Jews would bow. In attenuated form this may still be said of the Jewish people some 2,500 years later. Regretfully, though, not all national characteristics were eliminated or even tempered while they endured captivity. Constant complaining, a pronounced indolence and indifferent to serving God and each other and official corruption remained key elements in the Jewish character. (These assertions are forwarded with a bit of hesitancy since they can easily be said to mark any people at any time, but here our comments are limited to the historical record of the Jews alone).

EZRA

The Jews who returned from exile did not comprise a single amorphous glob of humanity, and like all they required leadership. Judah's most prominent postexilic leader and one of its historical best was Ezra, a priest in the line of Aaron and himself a trusted official in the Persian government of King Cyrus. Ezra's responsibility was enormous, and his problems would be a match for his power. The Jews, still a part of the Persian Empire, were home and at least to this point they were receiving not difficulty, but great support from Persia. It was Cyrus who was both sponsoring and financially supporting the reconstruction of the Temple, the first major task and one now entrusted to Ezra. It is common historical and popular knowledge that no construction project ever proceeds with smoothness, and the Temple's reconstruction fit well with that pattern. The Temple was important, but its immediacy of necessity was surpassed by the more important acts of worship. Soon after the return the people of Judah gathered together in Jerusalem and continually offered burnt offerings to God, as required by the Law of Moses. This was one of the few deprivations of freedom which had been made by the Persians, but now it could begin again. The scene in Jerusalem, though, was not one of undiluted satisfaction and joy, for the Temple, even to its foundation, still lay in ruins.

Six months would pass before work on the Temple began in earnest. The king's underwriting of the project, the people's contributions and the labor of men twenty and older finally completed the foundation of the building, and as the Jews were always wont to do a great celebration ensued and "... they sang together in praising and giving thanks to God... all the people shouted with a great shout, when they praised the Lord, because the foundation of the house of the Lord was laid." Great, even rapturous joy was the song of the day, for to the Jews "Israel was back." Still, if ever the word "bittersweet" is appropriate to an occasion here we find its natural home, as Ezra himself now relates:

> "But many of the priests and Levites and chief of the fathers,
> who were ancient men,
> that had seen the first house,
> when the foundation of this house was laid before their eyes,
> wept with a loud voice, and many shouted for joy."

The past evokes such beautiful yet haunting memories upon each of us, yet as our years accumulate those same glorious memories may conceal daggers of torture. The old men remembered how glorious was the ancient temple and the glory of Israel in its earlier and greater days, all of which darkly shadowed the joy of a reconstruction of a new, but far less impressive temple. As it so often does, Israel's present seemed to be hidden in the recesses of its past glories, as the new smaller temple so starkly reminded all.

Not only do building projects seem to inexorably attract the deleterious effects and elements of nature so do they often act as a magnet for human opposition and disfavor. So, too, did the reconstruction of the Temple. The northern neighbors of the Jews, whom we know as Samaritans, wanted to be "in on the action" and contribute to the building of the new Temple. In the marvelously descriptive language of the Old Testament the Samaritans are referenced as the "adversaries of Judah and Benjamin." The leading lights of Samaria came to the leader of the Jews, Zerubbabel, and offered their services as fellow servants of "your God," but they were rebuffed by the Jewish leaders, who claimed an exclusivity in this task. Before the modern woke twenty-first century reader castigates the Jews for their supposed narrow-mindedness let us recognize that the Samaritans effectively remained half-pagan and a Jewish union with them would be morally calamitous to the Jews.

The Samaritans did not recoil passively to being shut out of the building project, and they reacted to the Jews with two lines of attack. First, Ezra states simply but with language of enticing interest:

> "Then the people of the land (i.e. Samaria) weakened the hands of the people of Judah,
> and troubled them in building."

Secondly, and to many modern observers the Samaritans engaged in an even more dastardly act. The retained lawyers to advance their case, or as the ascriptive records they "...hired counselors against them" to make a case before the current Persian king, Ahasuerus (a man whom we shall see later becomes immortalized in history as Xerxes, to which he will hereafter be referred). The Samaritan's argument to Xerxes essentially became one of the perils that the Jews were gradually breaking away from the Persian Empire and with the reconstructed Temple would set themselves apart even further. Modern politicians, lobbyists, and the propagandizing media should take heart at the success (albeit temporary) of what is now called a "campaign of disinformation," for the king allowed the Samaritan advocates to convince him that the Jews were fermenting a rebellion with the reconstruction of the Temple. The Persian king, now a man named Artaxerxes, succumbed to the Samaritan argument that the Jews were seditious and were planning an insurrection. His response was the following:

> "I (the king) commanded,
> and search hath been made,
> and it is found that this city of old time
> hath made insurrection against kings,
> and that rebellion and sedition have been made therein."

The royal decree continued in this same light until the following hit as a thunderbolt:

> "Give ye now commandment to cause these men to cease,
> and that the city be not builded,
> until another commandment shall be given from me."

The king's final statement is a priceless pearl of political wisdom when he opined "... why should damage grow to the hurt of kings?" In the vernacular, "it is better to be safe than sorry" and of course, always, and ever – I, the king, must look out for myself. So, work on the Great Temple was suspended. Years later, under a new king of Persia, Darius, the Temple construction was recommenced and finally completed. Buildings, even great, beautiful, religious temples, and cathedrals come and go. At the time of this writing the burning destruction of much of the Notre Dame Cathedral in Paris remains a fresh memory, but likely it will be rebuilt, but whether its architectural beauty and magnificence restored remains open to question. The most lasting repercussion of the struggle to rebuild the Temple was the lasting enmity between the Jews and Samaritans, at first nourished by the latter and later replenished by other conflicts. It was a schism that not even the Savior centuries later was able to fully heal.

NEHEMIAH

For certain the Temple had been rebuilt, but a city's population cannot live in a Temple. The walls of Jerusalem had crumbled and long lay in ruins, making the city unsafe and open to attack. In Persia, a Jew named Nehemiah was troubled by this. Nehemiah, much as Daniel before, had risen from obscurity to high position in the royal palace as cupbearer to King Artaxerxes. Also as was Daniel, Nehemiah was highly valued by the king, and Nehemiah willingly, likely even with ardent enthusiasm, accepted a commission as royal governor of Judah. First on his list of priorities was a reconstruction of the city walls of Jerusalem, not for aesthetic purposes but rather that the city could be safely repopulated. Nehemiah was accorded great authority, much needed, for he found the leadership of Judah lacking and the people indolent. No longer could the Samaritans be blamed, nor did the Persian monarchy hinder the project. Actually, in point of fact the Persians were supportive. Nehemiah knew that the dearth of construction was due to the intransigence of the Jewish leaders and the protracted indolence of the people. The governor painted a grim portrait of the City of David when he pronounced:

> "(Y)e see the distress that we are in,
> how Jerusalem lieth waste,
> and the gates thereof are burned with fire:
> come, and let us build up the wall of Jerusalem,
> that we be no more a reproach."

The people responded favorably and even the priesthood, including the high priest responded with favor, the city walls were constructed, and Jerusalem became a revitalized city. More importantly, Nehemiah and Ezra worked together and a great revival of the people's faith in God and practice of religion spread.

Ezra and Nehemiah, although each is the author of an Old Testament history which bears his name, are easily overlooked and obscured men in the traditional pantheon of Old Testament greats. Nonetheless, overall, their efforts were highly productive, and the remnant had been reconstituted into a new nation. Ezra's death in circa 440 B.C. and Nehemiah's in circa 424 B.C. marked the passing of two men who accomplished much and with a minimum of historical and scholarly fanfare.

MALACHI

Before the closing of the Old Testament one voice remained to be heard, and this was of the prophet Malachi. This man easily merits the nomenclature of the "unknown prophet," for this basically is what he was. From the internal context of the book which bears his name our final prophet and chronicler of the Jews appears to have written his work about 400 B.C. Malachi had the pleasure of writing to a people who had finally turned to the monotheistic worship of the one true God, and the usual upbraiding about idolatry is absent from his work. Nonetheless, he saw massive problems which remained among the Jewish people. While for the first time in generations no foreign power directed their daily lives nor in any manner proscribed their religious practices the Jews began to settle into old, even some repulsive ways.

They made their sacrifices not to Baal, but to the God of Moses, but many of their sacrifices proved disgusting. On the altars were placed offerings of diseased animals, some blind, the weakest of herds and flocks, giving every proof that most Jews were just "going through the motions" of their religion. As such these newly freed Jews had sunk into a pit that never has, and never will, cease to plague sincere, true religion, i.e., legalistic formalism totaling lacking in the committed heart of its practitioner. Through Malachi God turned to the priesthood, the men who were complicit in accepting the corrupt sacrifices and prefaced His remarks with the attention getter of "O ye priests, this commandment is for you." A nakedly stark warning is given the priests and concludes with a starkness of language never equaled in the Bible for the bluntness of its imagery:

> "Behold, I will corrupt your seed,
> and spread dung upon your faces,
> even the dung of your solemn feasts;
> and one shall take you away with it."

(Contrary to the popular beliefs of many cynical disbelievers the Bible is not a collection of children's fairy tales, Puritanic morality plays and Victorian poetry). Although the names of pagan deities were no longer howled from the lips of the clergy, perhaps God was more incensed by their present behavior, in that they were mocking Him.

No practice of the Jews more pricked the God or roused the opposition of His chosen leaders, including first Ezra and Nehemiah, and now Malachi, than the practice of the Jews, increasingly common and accepted of their intermarriage with Gentiles. God, who created every race and each man and woman who ever lived, in modern terminology, not a "racist." Centuries later this truth was settled forever when Christ died for all, but not before speaking the words "for there is neither Jew nor Greek, for all are one with Christ." What concerned God, so presciently is the centrality of the truth that more often than not the Gentile spouses would turn the Jews away from God and back into idolatry. It was and remains a great concern of God.

Before we refocus the lens of our camera upon other nations and other people Malachi's remark on the then current attitude of the returned Jewish exiles is appropriate:

> "Ye have said,
> It is vain to serve God,
> and what profit is it that we have kept his ordinance,
> and that we have walked mournfully before the Lord of hosts?
>
> And now we call the proud happy;
> yea, they that work wickedness are set up;
> yea, they that tempt God are even delivered."

Gradually, but inexorably they were sliding back into the old and comfortable habits of indifference and ingratitude. Still, among this returning remnant was an even smaller, but faithful remnant and from their descendants would rise two and a half centuries hence the greatest moment in Jewish nationalist history. Yet, for now the small Jewish nation is relegated to the sidelines, and the pivot of history finds its epicenter among strange, heretofore "non-Biblical" places and persons. The Old Testament closes and scripturally until an angel appears to an obscure aging Jewish priest the rest is silence.

Not so for others, though, as now history and its observers affix the gaze upon the Gentiles.

CHAPTER TWO – THE UNSTOPPABLE PERSIAN TIDE

The Persian Empire was a glorious kingdom, the likes of which the world had never seen and has rarely glimpsed even to the present day. In the early fifth century (i.e. 400's) B.C., its king Ahasuerus ("Xerxes" hereafter) reigned over a kingdom:

> "...from India even unto Ethiopia, over a hundred and seven and twenty provinces."

So says the Hebrew Bible which coincides precisely with secular records, but it was not Xerxes that formed this behemoth of earthly sovereignty. It had required generations of conquests, alliances, treaties, work, and intent, but by the reign of the father of Xerxes, King Darius, in the 490's B.C. it was unmatched and unchallenged for supremacy. The tiny Jewish state of Israel, militarily unimportant, was of no reckoning when measuring power. The once feared empires of Babylon and Assyria had been beaten and subsumed by Persia and its armies. In the West, far, far away in the middle of the Italian Peninsula lay the small city of Rome, a Latin community still feeling its young way into what would be a majestic reckoning in history.

Spread over three continents and thousands of miles span the diversity of its people, races and cultures was enough to warm the heart of even the most exacting diversity compliance officer at the trendiest twenty-first century leftwing university. Persians, various Arabs, Jews, Indians, Kurds, the people from what is now southern Russia, the aforementioned Babylonians and Assyrians, and Ethiopians ad infinitum compiled the uncalculated populace of Persia. In the far western reaches of the Empire were the scatterings of another people, not great in number but ultimately eclipsing the Persians in historical importance. In coastal cities of Asia Minor (now Turkey) and numerous Aegean islands in the sea to its west lived a fair number of colonists from the compact land of Greece in southeast Europe. They were a hearty, tough lot, marked by an obstreperous character and a self-confidence that often trespassed into the realms of arrogance. Although ethnic distinctions and generalizations are fraught with danger it is reasonable to assert that on the whole the Greeks were proud, at times hubristic, intelligent, and usually diligent and hard working. They bore more than a superficial resemblance to another group that is central to our study, the Jews.

Greece and Greek culture usually demand voluminous writing, but we will forego this and note two salient points central to the plot. Like many people they came to highly resent foreign conquest and influence but were so often fatally hindered in their plans and desires to do anything about it. This was often due to that second of pertinent points, the seemingly natural diversity of the Greeks. Persia was not only a nation, but an empire, as were Babylonia and Assyria. Even the Jews could account for some unity at various times. The Greeks, though, seemingly could not abide their fellows and continually quibbled, tussled, and even engaged in brutal wars of revenge and conquest with one another. Their only loyalty was to the city-state, a unit of large, even massive numbers throughout this land of the Hellenes. As with many entities, though, especially families and nations, an existential crisis will either widen the rift or bring the parties closer. In 499 B.C. that crisis arrived.

One of the more underreported and less studied wars of ancient history was the Ionian Revolt. The Ionians were Greeks who lived along the central portion of the western coast of Asia Minor, still, of course, a province in the Persian Empire. The Ionians grew restless and increasingly hostile to their far-away masters when the Persians placed two tyrants, Histiaeus and Aristagoras, over them, as their rulers. Even for ancient Greeks the Ionians could be particularly truculent, and their revolt erupted into outright armed rebellion in 499 B.C. The rebellion quickly spread throughout other Greek dominated regions, including Cyprus, Aeolus, Eritrea, Caria, and Doria. Most importantly of all the second greatest military power and the greatest naval power of Greece, the city of Athens, lent its support, financial, military, and naval to the Ionians. The wars with numerous battles, the description of which along with the wars ebb and flow are not here pertinent, and the war raged for six years until the rebels suffered the ignominy of defeat and reconquest. The Persians had been quite successful and in their extinguishment of the rebellion, even adding new Greek territory to the empire. The rebellious Greeks were harshly punished, and the Persian dominance broadened, tightened, and deepened. Soon only one deed was left undone, the punishment of the "mainland" Greeks, especially Athens, which had with little reluctance engaged the mighty Persians.

Certainly, Athens was due its turn under the Persian lash, but what retribution would the Persians seek from these stiff-necked Greeks? By 490 B.C. King Darius had determined the course of his empire, and the direction and scope of the retribution he intended to exact from the Greeks was worthy of his throne. Darius organized a huge army ranging, according to various sources, from 70,000 to 100,000 men, who would be led west to supplement the empire and consolidate what he already controlled. Raising such a force, especially in ancient days, was a gargantuan task. Undoubtedly many of the soldiers were non-Persian, perhaps even various conscripted in nationalities, but the army of Darius was formidable, not just in size but in fighting skill. The king's famed "Immortals," his elite personal army and cavalry, reputed to be the best in the world, along with sheer mass of numbers made his army seemingly unconquerable.

The military history of the Ionian Revolt is long and intricate, and its understanding is not a sine qua non for what followed between the Persians and Greeks. A salient point or two, though, is certainly worthy of mention. First, it took far longer for the Persians to subdue a ragtag grouping of Greeks than they doubtless ever contemplated. Six years – a time surpassing that of either of the twentieth century's world wars, before the Persians had reestablished their full sovereignty and power over this unusual ethnicity. Long, protracted wars give birth to other emotions, many of them violent and often deplorable. Darius had "wasted" time, resources, and troops in subduing a people who to his royal Persian thinking should have been grateful to have him as their ruling monarch. A spirit of disciplinary retribution and outright additional ambition for more conquest arose within the bosom of Darius. Someone had to pay, and naturally they who "had to be taught a lesson" were the Greeks themselves, the mainland Greeks and most especially that city-state which had become the obloquy of Persia, Athens. The great conflict between Persia and Greece, a clash which would not only decide a battlefield victor, but which would direct the course of empires, civilizations and perhaps even manifest the hand and will of the Deity, was not over. In fact, it had not yet reached its half-way mark, but one of its dramatic zeniths was on the horizon.

THE PLAIN OF MARATHON

The immortal words of Shakespeare's King Henry V to his bedraggled English troops:

"Once more into the breach, dear friends, once more,
  Or close up the walls with our English dead."

It would be two millennia before the great poet would coin this inspiring phrase, but they could easily, with the replacement of English with Persian, been on the lips of Darius as he dispatched another vast army to Europe to subdue these intransigent Greeks. Not just an army, though, but a magnificent navy commanded by Artaphernes and Datis crossed the Aegean Sea and in July 490 B.C. the Persian forces captured the cities of Euboea and Eritrea. Now, the prize fruit of Athens was hanging low, ripe for the picking. The Persian forces sailed southward to Attica and landed in the bay near the town of Marathon, approximately thirty miles from Athens. In that Greek metropolis the army's commander, Miltiades, knew that the larger Persian force was ready and eager to destroy the Athenians, so Miltiades dispatched a messenger to Sparta, the premier Greek military power and without whom it remained doubtful that the small Greek force of Athenians and some soldiers from the small city of Plataea could withstand the blows from the Persians. No help would come from Sparta, though, a strange state with strange customs and even stranger men, all of whom were now engaged in a religious festival which had to be honored with their attendance. Miltiades received the devastating news, but regardless marched his force of perhaps 10,000 Greek hoplites to meet the Persian army of some 25,000 to 30,000, all to be arrayed on the Plain of Marathon in September 10, 490 B.C.

A strange word is "hoplite." A hoplite was a Greek citizen-soldier, in our current case an Athenian or Plataean property owner, who had a real stake in his city. He was a landowner, an artisan or other, but most importantly he had a real, vested, personal interest in the cause for which he was fighting. Helmeted, likely wearing a breastplate, and carrying a wooden shield on his right hand and a sword in his left he fought in a tightly packed phalanx with his fellow hoplites. An army of

10,000 Greek hoplites was indeed formidable. The Persians, in numbers two to three times greater than the Greeks, were no pushover, but man for man the Greek hoplites were superior.

The two armies came to grips in a battle which has few superiors in the number of extensive and in-depth historical chronicling it has drawn. We have no desire or ability to add to the historical record, and merely note that by a masterfully executed double envelopment Miltiades caused the Persians to retreat, leaving the bloodied field in the possession of the Greeks. The still large and dangerous Persian army retreated to the safety of their ships in the harbor. The Battle of Marathon had been won by the seemingly outclassed and outnumbered Athenians, with Greek and western civilization, then in its infancy, saved. For thousands of years Marathon has been accounted one of the most important battles in all human history. Its ability to draw interest and its overriding importance were perhaps most famously recognized by the English historian Sir Edward Creasy, who in 1851 authored the hugely popular, even yet today, <u>The Fifteen Decisive Battles of the World</u>, in which the first entry was the Battle of Marathon. Before that fateful plain passes totally from our gaze we concur that no retelling of Marathon is complete without the story of Pheidippides.

As the Persians withdrew from Marathon, the general Miltiades was not yet ready to inhale the exhilarating air of victory. He knew that the mighty Persian force could sail and outflank his small army and possibly march on Athens, an unfortified and lightly defended city. To ensure that the Athenians did not surrender before Miltiades and his army arrived, he dispatched Pheidippides, a man considered the swiftest runner in all Greece. Earlier in the week it was Pheidippides who raced the distance to Sparta and returned with the sad message that the Spartans were sending no help. Now, this prized athlete's task was to assure the Athenians that Miltiades and his army were coming and neither to despair nor surrender. Off, this magnificent but wearied runner sped, but mile after mile of torturous terrain wearied and began to break down his already over extended heart. Finally, he staggered the last few steps of his twenty-six-mile trip of torture into Athens and as he collapsed gasped his last words "We have ... victory!" He was dead, but Athens lived, and so did the memory of Pheidippides in a statue on that once embattled plain. It lives, too, throughout the world of today in the ever popular twenty-six mile plus distance race known as ...the "Marathon."

The Persian forces of Darius were beaten on the battlefield, and his army retreated to the safety of the Empire's borders. Although the Greeks, primarily the hoplites of Athens and Plataea had won an historic and magnificent triumph, the forces of Darius were hardly in disarray. Stung and deeply chagrined by unaccustomed defeat the king began to regroup and consolidate his forces for a new, even greater invasion of the Hellenic mainland of these upstart Greeks. As Politics, the affairs of kings and empires and life itself proceeds, though, events intervene. A major rebellion broke out in Egypt, and the Persians were forced to devote time, money, resources, and men to its eventually successful suppression. Then King Darius suffered the ultimate intervention in 486 B.C. when he died, leaving unfulfilled his plan to conquer Greece. His memory, though, was honored and upheld by his son Xerxes, a worthy successor, and a man eager to surpass his father's accomplishments.

Upon his assumption of the throne Xerxes was a young man upon his obtaining power he was thirty-two years old, still in his youthful prime but old enough to have shaken off the various weaknesses and detritus of life that plague young men. He was tall, described as handsome and an expert horseman, a once greatly admired skill in those days before mechanical transportation. Xerxes was infused with a more than healthy dose of monarchial ambition and a desire to rectify his father's failures and to expand the Empire even more. This time these strange recalcitrant Greeks would fall and would assume their properly ordained billets as provinces of the Persian Empire. In fact, a few Greek cities, and areas, among them Thessaly Argos and Boeotia, had already come over to the Persian side without the necessity of battle.

The early Greek chronicler of these events, Herodotus, the acclaimed "Father of History" wrote that Xerxes had gathered an invasion force of one million men, a number in the realm of fantasy, that has been reduced to 200,000 to 300,000 soldiers by later students. Those numbers still stagger the imagination, but it should not be forgotten that the Persian monarch had an enormous realm of 127 provinces from which to draw troops. In 480 B.C., with Xerxes accompanying his vast horde they marched westward to Greece. A large, unquantifiable number of soldiers were transported by an enormous fleet of perhaps one thousand ships, captained and manned primarily by Phoenician and Greek sailors. Overall, it was a martial movement of a scope the world had never seen, and all this for the small rocky land which was home to the ceaseless quibbling and internecine warfare of the Hellenes.

This time the Greeks knew the Persians were coming, but knowledge alone does not confer success. In the autumn of 481 B.C. representatives of those city-states which were committed to resisting the Persians met at the congress of Corinth, on that isthmus of land which connects northern and southern Greece. Many cities were represented, but only two cities were dominant, Athens and Sparta. The Athenians, of course, had already fought and bested the Persians at Marathon, but they were and still are more renown for their cultural, intellectual, governmental, and artistic achievements than for martial prowess. Sparta, lying at the southern portion of the Peloponnese, the great southern block of mainland Greece, was as distant in geography and in spirit from Athens as two cities, both Greek, and many learned students would aver that it was the best military force anywhere and at any time in history. Athens, as noted before, was a naval power.

To stop the Persians, it would require the forces and the cooperative leadership of Athens and Sparta, two cities extremely wary of one another. Even with a smoothly functioning union of Greeks it remains highly questionable whether the Persians could be stopped. But they would try.

Discussions, debates, and diatribes occupied the Greeks at Corinth, but eventually a strategy was adopted. With the storied Spartan infantry in the vanguard Greek troops would move as far northward as possible, in reality not to defeat the Persians but to delay them so that a larger more unified force could meet them farther south. The leader of the Athenians, a highly experienced (and in the eyes of his detractors a highly corrupt) statesman was Themistocles, who was also the admiral of the Athenian army, the force most likely to have any chance to defeat the Persians. It was determined that a contingent of Spartan troops led by its own king, Leonidas, joined by small contingents from Thespiae and other cities would march to Thermopylae in northern Greece and detain the Persian monstrosity as long as possible. But what was Thermopylae and really, what or who were the Spartans and Sparta? Thermopylae was nothing more than a small mountain pass in a rough mountainous region of northern Greece best described as semi-barbaric. In Greek, the name means "hot gates," so described for the hot sulphur springs nearly, which according to Greek mythology are the gates to Hades (or Hell) itself. It lies on the Gulf of Mahlis, itself a part of the Euripus Channel of the Argean Sea which forms much of the eastern border of Greece. The pass at Thermopylae was a narrow strip of land, perhaps no more than fifty feet wide which separated the water on the east from the steep mountains on the west. For ancient infantry it was superbly fashioned for defense. This defense was composed of tiny contingents from several Greek cities, but was led by a mere three hundred Spartans, the most feared and most professional warriors of antiquity and perhaps the most idealized in all history as perfect fighting machines. Still, why were they so few in number and what made them so special?

The Spartans were sui generis, one of a kind, and no matter the identity of the claimants nor their presumptive martial glory no nation or army since has ever matched the forces from this Greek city state in the Peloponnese, the southern mainland of Greece. Sparta seemingly developed separate and apart from the remainder of Greece. It was a highly and rigidly stratified society, and its population allocated to three classes. The upper, consisting of perhaps only 10%, were the full citizens, with all the rights, duties, and privileges of citizenry. The middle class, known as the periocci, comprised 20-30% of the state, and the helots, essentially a synonym for slaves the bulk of 60%-70%. Only the citizens were the soldiers, and historians have estimated that even at its heighth Sparta could field only a few thousand fighting men. Yet these soldiers were different from other Greek hoplites and pronouncedly different from other of history's martial forces. At age seven a Spartan boy was taken from his family and become the property of the state. He lived for years in rough, unheated barracks with his fellows and was brutally and arbitrarily treated to toughen him against the elements and to learn to disregard pain. His basic diet was a type of black broth or soup, repulsive to other Greeks. The child and then the youth was regularly beaten, not just for punishment but to inure him to hardship. Drill, endless ferocious drill as a member of a phalanx helped perfect him as a soldier non-pareil. He was taught that death in battle was the highest virtue, but as a member of the maltreated Spartan elite he was encouraged to lie, steal, and cheat. Few they were in number (echoes of "the Marines are looking for a few good men") his life was t he definition of "hard," his discipline in battle unmatched and his reputation of gigantic size. At that narrow pass at Thermopylae King Leonidas commanded but 300 Spartans to hold back the tide of Persia and to save the nascent civilization of Greece in its infancy. Only 300? The Spartans were engaged in a religious festival at the time, and its ruling oligarchy forbade its soldiers to leave Sparta for its duration. The 300 comprised the King's personal bodyguard, who were subject to his orders only. It was a miniscule and a strange contingent that for two days held the pass at Thermopylae against the teeming hordes from Persia, but hold they did, all the time each hour buying time for the other Greeks, primarily the Athenians, to prepare for the Persian onslaught.

On the third day, a Greek known only by his name of Ephialtes got word to King Xerxes of a narrow trail through the mountains by which the Persians could pass and outflank the Spartans from the rear. For his traitorous efforts Ephialtes was well rewarded with Persian gold, and the Spartans, surrounded by the enemy, were slain to a man. When the last of the three hundred expired a legend, as bright today as ever, was born. It was a legend, unlike some, the examination of which upholds its inspirational truth. These strange men, hardened soldiers to the core, contemptuous of art, gentleness, and kindness, and knowing little of freedom in their own lives had made a classic last stand, perhaps history's greatest, for freedom, individuality and in an increasingly recognizable fashion the truths of the God of the Bible. At those "hot gates" to Hell on a late summer day in 480 B.C. Western civilization was saved.

But the plaudits and sentimentality of our present were not on the minds of the mass of Greece that day. The Persians had broken through the outer defenses, and all Greece lay before them. Under the leadership of Athens and Themistocles the Greek forces withdrew southward, with much of the Persian strength following asea in the massive navy which sewed the whims of Xerxes. Themistocles, both politician and the Athenian admiral skillfully lured the massive Persian fleet of as many as 1200 ships into the Straits of Salamis, a narrow strait of water to the southwest of Athens. Themistocles opposing forces have been estimated in the range of one-third to one-half of that possessed by Xerxes. The naval action, as so much combat at sea historically has been wars fought close to shore, and on a hillside overlooking the battlefield of water Xerxes sat on his marble throne for a prized view of his fleet destroying the Greeks and granting him Greece and its civilization. The very model of an Oriental potentate in all his luxury, finery and hubris Xerxes watched the battle unfold and his dreams of a European empire begin their collapse. Themistocles had skillfully drawn the Persians into the narrow straits and shallow waters and had administered to the mighty Persians a sever drubbing on this September 480 B.C. day. Both a megalomaniac and a realist Xerxes knew the poor, rocky land of Greece could not support his army so with one-half his forces the great king of Persia returned to his homeland.

Only one-half, though, so one-half remained to trod the soil of Greece. Finally, one year later in August 479 B.C. under the leadership of Sparta the Greek forces came to grips once again with the Persians and soundly defeated them at the Battle of Plataea. Never again would Persia seriously threaten Greece.

It has become de rigueur in these early days of the twenty-first century to dismiss with a startling sneer ranging between bitter humor and outright hatred the very concept of Western civilization, and perhaps no where more stridently than its longtime religion of Christianity. To many it is seen as passé, misguided to some and the embodiment of evil to others. What had those Spartans at Thermopylae, Athenians at Salamis is and so many Greeks at Plataea rescued from oblivion? It certainly was not Christianity, which was centuries in the future. It is likely that in this fifth century B.C. it would have been difficult, well nigh impossible to find a Greek or a Persian who had even heard of the Hebrew God. What was saved and what, if any role, did God assume in the process of history. The ensuing chapters will address both questions.

CHAPTER THREE – THE GLORY THAT WAS GREECE

Twice within the span of a decade the Persian tide had reached the shores of Greece. The first was a strong current led by Darius, but it was repelled by the skill and courage of the Athenians. The second in 480 B.C. was a tsunami, which from the retrospective perch of two and one-half millennia excites wonder, admiration, and almost but not quite, disbelief. Four battles were fought against the hordes of Persia and facing overwhelming odds the Hellenic army and navy triumphed in the final three. Yet it was the lone defeat in the pass at Thermopylae that has echoed throughout history, a reverberation of heroism, determination, and the acceptance of certain death so that Greece and its historical progeny, Western civilization, would live. Almost of a certainty, though, when those Spartans exhaled their final breaths, they so did oblivious to any awareness of such an entity as "Western civilization." It is time to examine how and just what was saved by the deaths of a relatively few Greeks at Marathon, Salamis, Plataea, and of course, most famously, Thermopylae.

As to the "how" of the inquiry the defeated Persians must ever be considered. The massive polyglot empire of the Persians would remain not only viable, but also, vibrant. Its days of Greek invasions were over, though, as it turned elsewhere and also inward. Persia, as we will see, would reappear as a massive and forceful entity in Greek history a century and a half later, but its days as an invader of the small Hellenic state at the extreme southeastern corner of Europe were over. Small as it may have been, the native Greeks had Greece to themselves, and in a purely cultural and intellectual sense no nationality has ever made more of the opportunities for peaceable production.

As it did in war Athens led the way forward in peace. The number of Greek city-states, large and small, was astounding for a land mass as small as Greece and the equally small population which it bore. Sparta was a negligible naval power, but the superior to Athens and all Greek cities militarily. Yet in the cultural glory of Greece, it was a non-entity, even a willing nonentity, for its military prowess seemed to satiate the Spartans' thirst for glory and honors.

A history of ancient Greek cultural development requires a panel of multi-discipline scholars whose product would threaten the stability of the strongest bookshelf. Even a summary of what the Greeks (centered in Athens) discovered, wrote, and created is beyond the scope of a single small volume, so ours will be little more than an impressionistic glance at the fruits of the glory that was Greece, the phrase coined by the nineteenth century American poet Edgar Allen Poe (yes, that Poe). Actually, the Greeks may have "invented," little, but in the creative phase of the development of the arts and sciences, they are unsurpassed, perhaps even into the present century. In medicine, a science still in its embryonic stages, at least two names live yet today, the physicians, Galen and Hippocrates, the "Father of Medicine" himself. The latter especially organized the discipline of medicine and presented a structural, medical, and moral basis for its good and legitimate practitioners in the phrase "First, do no harm." Even in the hands of men of intellect and good will in antiquity medicine was a primitive practice, but a great step forward was made by the early Greek legends.

Since medicine and law, as are doctors and lawyers, often yoked together in phraseology (actually for no apparent good reason) our gaze lights on the legal system. It would be not just an overstatement but rather a misstatement to aver that the Greeks invented any modern Western legal system. By the time of their rise to prominence in any nations had already developed a jurisprudence of some complexity, none more than the Hebrews, who had received the Law of Moses from God Himself. Its scope and detail, and the exactitude of its pronouncements have never been surpassed. As any student of the Bible knows, though, its overriding purpose was theological and moral. Where the Greeks began to excel, especially in the 300's B.C. was in the development of laws regulating such as governmental administration, contracts, and an extensive criminal code. In continental Europe it later became the Roman legal code which became the template for the laws of its nations, but the Greeks had broken the legal ground.

The art (or is it science?) of architecture is a study and profession for which the Greeks of old have left their greatest physical imprint. Certain architectural styles, not limited to the ancients, were practiced and nearly perfected by the ancient Greeks. As schools have long taught, often to the transient memory of their students, ancient Greek architecture was divided into three basic systems, the Doric, Ionian, and Corinthian. The imagery of spectacular columns in buildings such as the Parthenon is lasting to the present. Even in this self-proclaimed post-modern age many structures retain noticeably classic designs.

The various artistic endeavors and achievements of the ancient Greeks still excite wonder and administration. Unfortunately, certain works have been lost or destroyed, especially works of sculpture, which have suffered from the elements, theft, looting, foreign invasion, and purposeful destruction. The Greeks and their admiring artistic descendants, though, found much to applaud in the works of sculptors with names such as Myron, Phidias, Polyclitus, Praxiteles, Scopas, and Lysippus.

Seemingly without cessation might we chronicle and commemorate the accomplishments of the ancient Greeks in both the arts and the sciences. A fair question, though, is whether they produced anything that was of joy, comfort or even entertainment to their contemporaries. Happily, the answer to such an inquiry would be a resounding yes. Among other achievements the ancient Greeks "invented" classical, which became Western, literature. We have placed the verb invented in quotation marks because it does not seem quite proper or accurate to declare any writing as having been invented. Perhaps more accurately it may be referenced as created and transcribed, but the Greeks's first great writer likely performed only the former. The practically unknown and uncelebrated blind Greek poet Homer wrote in the 700's B.C. Somehow his works were recorded, though, and to this moment in time they are read, celebrated, performed, filmed, reviewed, and analyzed. They are <u>The Odyssey</u> and <u>The Iliad</u>, both of which employ plot devices and characterizations that never become dated. Surely great numbers of Greeks enjoyed their reading, oral retelling or perhaps even their dramatic performance. What Homer began was followed and celebrated, and writers, historians, poets, dramatists, and playwrights followed in teeming numbers.

As we divide today, so did the Greeks, had penned their literary works in two distinct categories, what we now call fiction and nonfiction. We have mentioned Herodotus the great historian, who was followed by Xenophon and Thucydides, an Athenian who died in 399 B.C., the great scribe of the Hellenic civil war, whose History of the Peloponnesian War in eight volumes, has been proclaimed by numerous scholars as not only the greatest history of antiquity but also for those ancient days its greatest work of all literature. The ancient Greeks, though, different as they were from we moderns in language, dress, lifestyle, and countless other matters likely did not en masse spend any leisure time in the reading of history books. Wherein they and we have a shared identity was/is in the national enjoyment of dramatic presentation or plays.

Dramatic plays, with actors, scripts, dialogues, and various miscellany are yet performed from Broadway to the neighborhood elementary school. Within the lifetimes of this writing modern technology has boosted the audience for watching plays. The advent of radio, movies, television, the internet, and electronic devices beyond the ken of all but the most advanced technological wizard have brought the performance of the dramatic arts to every nook and cranny of the globe. It all began with the Greeks, the first to develop the disciplines of dramatic presentation, and who led the way with three great dramatists, Aeschylus, Euripides and Sophocles, whose plays are commonly performed today. If the reader has ever enjoyed a movie, a play or a television show the original source of the pleasure lies in the talents of the ancient Greeks.

In the realm of letters, among the ancient Greeks a trio of names was preeminent and are still predominant. Never have they been considered light reading, and actually the first of them wrote nothing at all. "Philosopher" is a word that is practically interchangeable with the names of Socrates, Plato, and Aristotle. They mused, spoke, and wrote upon human relationships, moral philosophy, and political theory to a depth that apart from a book which an obscure Semitic people known as the Hebrews had developed, was never known before. Rarely read but by academics, scholars and the occasional man or woman of an intellectual bent they added greatly to the glory that was Greece.

Never has such a small, poor, land produced the cultural riches as did Greece, and in the period following the culmination of the Persian Wars, the cultural and scientific fields of its efforts seemed to produce ever richer harvests. Greece was not an "overnight sensation," but rather was a long developing effervescent jewel, in many ways, a beautiful prism of glory. But in many ways, it was not. Creative, prideful, innovative they were, but these character traits were not confined to the mundane temporal arena of this world. The Greeks were highly inventive in matters of religion, and had a positive genius for creating deities, various gods and goddesses of which, in point of fact, remain interesting to study (and for Hollywood to make movies). Here, though, history compels us to admit that the genius of Greece was matched by the talents of other ancient pagan nations in create deities which they believed were worthy of worship. Our focus, though, remains upon the Greeks and momentarily at this work's juncture, upon their religion, or as now referenced Greek Mythology.

No quick summary of the ancient Greek religion is worthy of the paragraph or two it would require for its discussion. It was complex, fluid, subject to change and capable of adding gods and goddesses to its pantheon without a moment's hesitation. Nonetheless, its basic traditional form is worth an interested glance so that we become familiar with its basic structure. In the "ancient" days themselves of ancient Greece, the Greeks worshipped gods known as the Titans, a Greek mythological name which yet today retains a cachet for size, strength, and power. The Titans included the gods Atlas, Cronus, Oceanus, and Prometheus, each of whom had his separate realm of power and each of whom bears a name with modern familiarity. These were the deities of the antiquity of ancient Greece itself, and many had names which resonate yet today, including the strength of Atlas or the sufferings of Prometheus, who was tortured and chained to a rock. Their study may currently live with us yet today, but they had their expiration dates with the ancient Greeks, who eventually replaced these Titans with the gods and goddesses who dwelled on Mount Olympus, the deities most praised and feared by the Greeks and most studied by classicists thereafter. This grouping included Zeus, the chief of all gods, Hera, Poseidon, Athena, Apollo, Artemis, Aphrodite, Demeter, Dionysus, Ares, and Hera. These names are not chronicled out of a desire for historical tedium but rather to illustrate two essential points. The first is that the Hellenic religion was potent and interesting to names of so many of its gods and goddesses forever living in legend and mythology. The second is the illustration of their numbers, for this is but a sampling. Several centuries later the most famous apostle of a strikingly different religion had walked the storied streets of

Athens. Later, addressing the Athenian intelligentsia on Mars Hill he exclaimed:

> "For as I passed by and beheld your devotions,
> I found an altar with this inscription,
> "To the Unknown God,"
> whom therefore ye ignorantly worship..."

Greeks, especially what we would call the educated, or even the "pundit" class found it highly objectionable to be called ignorant by anyone, least of all a strange, itinerant Jew with an even stranger religious message. But it was all true. The Greek religion had no systemic structure, no underlying moral message, but rather it was a rambling, though at time highly fascinating, collection of wild stories, gods and goddesses of prodigious strengths, appetites, both carnal and sexual and of "moral" characteristics more to be eschewed than emulated. They had power struggles, marital infidelities and at times even the most prominent of them seemed to abide in a state of unquenched rage. The Greeks themselves noticed the gods, built them temples, designated priests and priestesses, and celebrated an ever-increasing number of holidays in their honor. Yet the essential elements of religion, "true religion" as the Holy Bible so defines it were lacking. These were the inseparable elements of moral integrity and service to God and to man. In the plainest of terms, the Greeks' religion seemed to have little effect upon the average personal conduct of any Greek and was (like many religions) honored more in name than in practice. Still, in those legendary contests with the Persian power of the East the free practice of the Greeks' religion did not perish. It was saved for centuries, but for what purpose and when end?

Actual morality, or more appropriately immorality, is often separated from religion, even among self-professedly "religious" persons, as were most of the ancient Greeks. The essential moral principles of what has been dubbed (somewhat awkwardly) the Judeo-Christian tradition include personal integrity, honesty, loyalty, kindness, respect, even deference to others, and above all humility. Most certainly, among the ancient Greeks these elements of virtue were practiced and could be found, but they were not the norm. Although concern for women was not absent totally from ancient Greece, and laws, literature and exemplary personal conduct could be found where women were protected, Greece was a man's world. Not all Greece was Sparta, but as one of its two leading states its political and moral ethic cannot be bypassed with closed eyes. Sparta was in the fore of a celebration of a culture of "manliness," and to some degree this was the source of admirable qualities. The military acumen and ferocity of the Spartan warrior reached mythical status, a status which shows no sign of diminution even well into the twenty-first century. Spartan prowess, so vital at Thermopylae was integral in keeping Greece of rid of Persian rule. It was the end product, though, of an unmerciful statist militarism which dragged seven-year-old boys from home and threw them into a hard, brutal, ultra-masculine arena for their childhoods, youth and well into adulthood. The miasmic militarism of Sparta produced soldiers non-pareil, but it was unnatural. Boys grew to men in a completely masculine environment, where the hardness and severity of character was developed, but so were other things. Sparta in particular and Greece as a whole developed a cult of masculinity, where most of the virtues of the Sermon in the Mount would have been contemptuously disregarded. For example, the virtues of modesty and humility, both integral and even foundational to the Biblical view of things had little place or purpose in ancient Greece. Braggadocio among men was deemed a masculine virtue, and many Greeks, including their greatest writers and artists, showed little hesitation in its practice.

This small rocky piece of earth, composed of its mainland and surrounding islands, if not unique in the purest definition of the word, was somewhat singular and a pioneer in the ancient world. Its artistic and scientific achievements still stagger a fair-minded observer. Their depth and breadth form a large part of the foundation of Western civilization. Yet, other shadows loomed over its Hellenic glory, and here our observations must be fitted into a timely place. For millennia Christendom (and other civilizations) deplored and condemned certain practices, which have become in the last generation or so not just accepted, but then approved and now celebrated. They include pedophilia and homosexuality, both of which were common, and at times even exalted, among the Greeks.

Greece was a small land, boasting but a modest population but fully beset with every vice and sin of this world, be it ancient or modern. It produced wise, far-sighted men and women as well as an abundant host of schemers, traitors, cutthroats, and hypocrites. Ancient Greece extended the frontiers of art, science, and philosophy, and so many nations and their citizens have thereafter built upon its foundation. Yet, what still makes Greece unique, especially for a culture that knew not God, was what for the lack of finer terminology we call "the spirit of free inquiry" in whatever discipline or study the Greek pursued. Art, sculpture, architecture, philosophy and much else glorify our impressions and memories of Greece. Yet, the arena where Greece, or at least Athens, lit a torchlight for centuries to follow, was in the realm of government.

Athens was not all Greece, and certainly not all Greece was this Attic city-state, a proud, increasingly self-glorifying entity, that developed concepts of government which are still honored today, though just as often in the breach as in the observance. A traditional text (increasingly rare) of the history of Western society, informs us that the Athenians developed democracy, or the rule of the people. The underlying premise is truthful, although Athens never practiced pure democracy, and likely no state since has done so. Even great Athens, depending on the time and era, had a continual flow of governments, ranging on the scale of despotism, dictatorship, oligarchy, military rule and even their version of democracy. What Athens unloosed was the idea that all citizens (usually limited to free males, though) had a right to participate in government decisions and even to argue and debate his position in an assembly of his peers. In other terms, the Athenian Greeks honored the principle of a discussion of free ideas, of giving each man a say in the determination of his own life. It was a principle that is a flowing stream throughout Western history, sometimes, perhaps even frequently squelched and trampled, but it is a headwater from which many of the ideas which permeate the West, its culture, its people, and its religion flow. Democracy has never been a panacea to solve the world's woes, but many of its principles have forwarded some of the better elements of society, and to the Greeks, however fumbling and awkward their manifestation of these ideas may have been, the West should remain grateful. Still, democracy is no glorious end in itself, but it allows for the flowering of individualism. This is not the individualism of selfishness or greed (which arise under any form of government) but more the individualism expressed in the justice of laws, individual civil rights, and a recognition of the worth of each person. Imperfect as it was and wholly unaware of the aptness of the comparison Greek democracy's ethic in some ways mirrored God's Law of Moses and the ultimate embodiment of justice in Christianity.

Ancient Greece, especially Athens, indeed was glorious in so many ways, but to borrow one of the still extant phrases from its own trove of ancient literature, Greece had its "Achilles heel." Capable of definition in so many ways it comes down to the basic truth that the Greeks simply could not get along with each other. Politically, "Greece" did not exist, but rather its political substance was a long roster of city-states, whose great raison d'tre seemingly was the joy of making shifting political alliances and internecine warfare that at times strikingly imitated a type of national self-genocide. The Greeks' internal destruction often revolved around its two polar opposites, Athens and

Sparta and the various municipalities that joined them as allies. It culminated in the Peloponnesian War, a generational long struggle from 430-402 B.C., where each side with their allies trampled across the hills, plains, and cities of Greece, brutalizing their fellow Greeks in a conflict which its greatest modern scribe described as "A War Like No Other." In its early years it was fought in the midst of a pandemic of plague centered in Athens, and the War's full casualty list is incalculable. So much for the idea that intellectual advancement and attainment is a shield against the outbreak of wars and human savagery. For the record, Sparta was the victor.

As in the aftermath of all wars matters finally returned to some form of normalcy, and so they did in Greece. Its society still produced amazingly gifted artists, scientists, and sculptors, but as a whole it was politically weakened. Along with Athens and Sparta, both of which the Peloponnesian War weakened, new city-states of power, most notably Corinth and Thebes arose in Greece. They would continue the civil unrest which seemed to be endemic to the land, but as the decades passed, Greece itself weakened, and by the mid 350's B.C. the eyes of the Hellenes began to turn northward where the greatest threat to Greece since the glory days of Persia was looming. A small semi barbaric kingdom and its two most famous individuals, a father and son, would change not only Greece but the paths of history forever. Also, by their actions and legacies they would move that small ship from our Introduction a bit closer to port.

CHAPTER FOUR – GOD'S GREAT SERVANTS

Macedonia has always suffered from an identity crisis. Depending upon the date of the map it will be shown as a Balkan country, whether part of another nation, most recently Yugoslavia, or the upper tier of Greece, or for hundreds if years a component of the Ottoman (Turkish) Empire. In our day, but always subject to the winds of political change, the northwestern third of Macedonia is an independent nation known as the Kingdom of North Macedonia while the remaining two-thirds is a part of the nation of Greece. Historically, it has always been a source of confusion, and no more so than when the question of ethnicity (always a hazard) is raised. Is Macedonia Greek or is it Slavic, as are almost all the other Balkan nations of southeastern Europe. Today we have no easy answer, and this situation is consistent with the Macedonia of the 400's and 300's B.C.

To the southern Greeks of ancient days, it was not a difficult question, for to them they were non-Greeks, and thus barbarians; however, the ancient Greek view is not alone dispositive of the question. For all their glory and accomplishments by the time on which we now focus the intelligentsia and the opinion-makers and influencers of the ancient Greeks. It is they that coined the word still prevalent today, "barbarian" to describe any person who was not a Greek. A Greek would mock a speaker of a non-Greek language with this term because to him the foreigner sounded as if he was just babbling the sounds of "bar-bar" repeatedly, hence the word "barbarian."

Greece's northern neighbors, the Macedonians, were different in at lease two ways. First, many of the Macedonians wished to identify themselves as Greek, and whatever their etymology it was entirely logical to do so. The Macedonians spoke Greek, albeit a heavily accented not easily discernible Greek to their southern neighbors. Toi the more conventional and in some cases urbane mainstream Greek, the Macedonian was at best a difficult to understand crude northern cousin, though a distant one. The view which the typical Judean Jew had of his northern kin in Galilee, a province of rustics, fishermen, carpenters, and the like comes to mind.

Greece of antiquity was never fertile ground for growth of monarchies. By the 300's B.C. Sparta, among the major city-states, clung to its kingly institutions. Being Sparta even monarchy here resided but with a special unusual Spartan twist. This great warrior kingdom simultaneously would maintain two kings, and how such a system could function remains perplexing. Mainland Greece's other outlier was its derided cousin to the north, Macedonia, which maintained its own royal line. In 383 B.C. there was born to the Macedonian King Amyntas and his wife Eurydice, a son, christened Philip II of Macedon, who would transform Macedonia and Greece and lay the foundations for the transformation of the world. (For reference and simplicity hereafter, he will be noted often only as Philip). Early in life, even as a small boy, Philip learned the needs and exigencies of ancient diplomacy. As a child he spent years in the Greek city of Thebes as a type of security for Theban rights and influence in Macedonia. In 359 B.C. he assumed the government of Macedonia, but he demonstrated that at the tender age of twenty-four he was meet for the job.

Unlike his soon to be more famous son we have little in the manner of a physical description of Philip. He is described as a mature man possessed of a thick, bushy brown beard, which itself would make him indistinguishable from the mass of Macedonian males. Our extant history, though, leads us to surmise that it is unlikely he sported the soft appearance of one borne to the purple, and tenderly and gently raised in a palace. Macedonia was poor, and from childhood Philip seemed to be involved in state affairs. Our story will reflect that he became an experienced soldier and suffered the loss of an eye in 354 B.C. at Methone. Philip was a highly intelligent man, a diligent worker and not particularly brutish in a brutal age. Events will show that he could think beyond the level of the battlefield, but he was certainly not the idealized "philosopher-king" of the eminent philosopher Plato. Philip was always a practical man who inevitably found the way to acquire what he wanted, whether it was Macedonia or his personal pleasure.

In so many manners Philip of Macedon demonstrated that he was both Greek and non-Greek. His ultimate life purpose seemed to be the spreading of not only his own personal Macedonian hegemony but Greek cultural attainments throughout the world. He was not a typical Greek ruler, though, in that unlike his Hellenic peers he joyfully practiced polygamy, having a total of seven wives. Monogamy was more the norm with the Greek ruling class, although that recognition in no manner should imply widespread marital fidelity. As was so common among the ancient Greek men Philip also took for himself numerous men and boys as lovers, all the while having the multiplicity of wives. (Where this is to be placed on the modern LGBTQ continuum is left to the individual reader's discretion).

Philip was a warrior, an intelligent, highly, skillful soldier and commander. He organized and commanded a force of superb skills and the equal of any in antiquity, the Macedonian Army. It was no untrained mob, as were so many ancient forces, but rather a superb fighting mechanism organized in the phalanx, a formation of men who fought in units eight rows deep. The structural concept was nothing new as the hoplites of the main Greek city-states had been fighting this way for years. What was new is that Philip armed his soldiers with pikes, the length, and sharp points of which made the Macedonian phalanx on its battlefield approach a bristling hedgehog of intimidation. It worked extraordinarily well, and many enemy formations crumpled and ran at its approach. The skilled soldiers who filled the ranks of the Macedonian and Greek phalanxes would well serve their countries and perhaps others well for generations.

As great a warrior and general as Philip established himself to be his skills as a statesmen and negotiator were no less formidable. Gradually he formed alliances with other city-states of Greece, and any isolation of Macedonia ended. The king was adept and ruling well what he controlled and had what very few politicians of if preferred statesmen, possess. That was a remarkable gift of knowing when to negotiate and when to take up arms against the enemy. Philip could destroy, but he preferred to build, both by alliances and then by consolidating what he had gained. He would wage war on whomever he deemed necessary, but peaceful victories were more to his taste. During his tenure he acquired Thrace and Thessaly, both of which enriched Macedonia considerably with their gold mines. With each as well as with many lesser Greek states his acquisition or territory was essentially peaceful, although Philip was a classic example of extending an iron hand covered by a silken glove. With him the threat of violence, the horrendous, grotesque violence of ancient warfare always loomed.

Our essay makes no pretense at a military study, but hopefully is successful in revealing the nature of this talented and ambitious king. Historically, as we have discussed two great cities dominated Greece, Athens, and Sparta. By the time that Philip invaded the Peloponnese in 338 B.C. Spartan territory and power had so evaporated that even without battle Spartan power came to its end. With Athens it was different, but with Athens everything was always different. Into the days of the rise of Philip and Macedonia Athens remained a great naval power, and its status in the fore of the Greek political structure rested in large measure on its control of the sea. It was not the nature of a man such as Philip II to cringe and bemoan his weaknesses in the face of strength. It was, though, his nature to perform with resolute action and to take up arms against the threatening foe. Yes, Athens was a great naval power, but where was it ordained, thought Philip, that it was the sole great naval power. Thus, the king committed the Macedonians to becoming a maritime power, succeeded in his efforts, and the great intimidating specter of Athenian naval power was blunted.

King Philip II of Macedonia had become the greatest and most threatening force ever developed in the small, combined land of Macedonia and Greece. No man or woman ever succeeds in acquiring universal fame, admiration, and adulation, and certainly Philip provided no exception. He had enemies, though they were customarily crushed by force of arms or neutralized by agreement and alliance, but Philip had only one Demosthenes. This Athenian statesman was the great orator of his day and in a place and an era in which a high premium was placed upon speech and oratory Demosthenes was considered the best. Still, he was much more than a man of words, and truly he was the enemy of Philip. Demosthenes apparently saw, with some reason, that Philip was a semi-barbarian interloper in Greek business. Although he might be greatly gifted, a great battlefield strategist and tactician and an accomplished diplomat, to Demosthenes he remained an outside interloper in Greek affairs. He did not remain silent, however. In a series of three, perhaps four, orations in Athens in the 340's B.C. he lambasted Philip and viewed him as an existential threat to Greece itself. The Macedonian king was excoriated by Demosthenes in the finest and fiercest oratory which the ancient Greeks had to offer. An alliance with Philip was unthinkable, Demosthenes spoke, and any subordination of Greek interests to Philip was suicidal. So powerful were these speeches they were copied three centuries later by that most famous of all ancient orators, the Roman Senator Cicero in his denunciation of a corrupt Roman name Catiline. To the present day the actions of Demosthenes and his denunciation of Philip were so powerful that the speeches themselves are know as the "Philippics." Alas, it was to no avail, though. Athens had one last throw of the dice remaining, and at the Battle of Chaeronea in 338 B.C. Philip's forces and those of Athens and a few of its allies met in combat. The Athenians fought with skill and ferocity, but eventually their forces were broken, and the battlefield hero of the day was none other than the eighteen-year-old son of Philip himself.

Macedonia under its seemingly unstoppable king was now the sole dominating force in Greece, yet Philip's goal with Greece (albeit under his dominance) was unity, and in a formal, legal manner such was soon established. The entity which was established was the League of Corinth, a Macedonian/Greek covenant made for the purposes of an invasion and war of conquest against Persia.

Macedonia and Greece, at least for an indeterminate future were inextricably aligned with one another, and it was the outlier, the rough king and kingdom from the north that was the dominant partner. In Philip's world and in his thoughts the stars were all aligning in his favor. Personally, he had some mileage and its marks upon him, but he still was a powerful man for all to consider. He was a proven genius of statecraft, a military innovator of success and a proven commander in battle. Added to the superb Macedonian phalanxes, which numbered upwards of 50,000 well trained soldiers was a large, but imprecisely calculable number of Greek hoplites. The world and its glories, outside Greece and Macedonia, awaited King Philip of Macedon, but first a moment of celebratory family pleasure beckoned the great, soon to be greater, monarch.

A wedding is always a big moment, but a royal wedding, especially in ancient times, was of special input. Philip, the husband of seven wives, and father to numerous sons and daughters was the most celebrated attendee on October 3, 336 B.C. at a wedding in Aegean, the ancient capital of Macedonia. His daughter Cleopatra (not that Cleopatra) was being wed to Alexander I (not that alexander) of Epirus. The wedding ceremony itself was complete, but unlike modern nuptials a wedding in ancient Greece, especially at this strata in society, was very much a male-dominated affair. Heavy drinking, coarseness of behavior, ribaldry and whatever were standard practice, especially at what we might tag the "reception" which followed. Philip, as much as any man present, was a willing and enthusiast participant, and his physical senses and awareness no doubt shrouded in drink. This was by no means a novelty, and the danger to the king was minimal, especially since he was accompanied by seven strong young bodyguards. One was Pausanias, who had long served Philip well. From boyhood to the strength of youth he had performed his duties well, both as security for the king's person and a favorite in the king's bed. Philip had moved on to others, though, so Pausanias, consumed with hatred and jealousy, plunged a knife into King Philip II, and with the scarlet blood flowing from him both Philip and his great plan of world conquest died. Pausanias, though he sought to escape, was quickly apprehended and in rage Philip's supporters killed the assassin. In a final coda of contempt, they crucified the body of Pausanias.

Although the threat of the sword underlay all the actions of Philip II of Macedon it cannot be denied and should not be overlooked that his skills, from whatever their source, were extraordinary. As a Macedonian outsider he did what no man before had done and brought a unity to Greece. He thus provided a template for other world conquerors, whose characters are even more stained than his. Much later the Corsican of Italian heritage, Napoleon Bonaparte, made the French Empire. Neither of those twin monsters of world dominance, Adolf Hitler or Joseph Stalin was native to the nation which he mobilized for death and conquest, Hitler being an Austrian in Germany and Stalin of Russia being from the obscure nation of Georgia.

The body of Philip was attended with the respect due not just a monarch but a man of superior talents by any measure. It was interred, lamented, and memorialized and his abilities and stature lauded and eulogized to the satisfaction of all. Still, after a lifetime's satiation of laurels, deeds, glories, and accomplishments King Philip II of Macedon was gone. But in the context of the strange, perhaps even quirky title of this chapter, in which his story has been briefly recounted how was Philip one of God's great servants? To history's knowledge he never traveled to Judah and knew nothing, likely to the point of an existential unawareness, of the existence of Judah's God. How then could Philip serve a God of whom he was unaware? Actually, this has never proven a formidable obstacle to the ever-reigning God of the universe, of which this small effort hopefully will provide a later and more complete analysis.

Before Philip Greece had the glories of its martial past, of Marathon, Salamis, and Plataea and a defeat at Thermopylae which history transformed into its greatest triumph. Yet, until now and with the notable exception of Sparta, Greece is really not to be recognized as one of history's great martial states. Its glory was the glory of the Divinely created mind and the accomplishments of well-directed thought, even theory, and tangible creative construction in the arts, science, engineering, ad infinitum. Philip himself was a politician and a general, enormously capable and accomplished in each sphere, and himself was no man of arts and letters. The life accomplishment of King Philip II was in bringing together, yes, often, through bloodshed, a long existing inchoate mass of city-states, all Greek, adding his own Macedonia to the mix, and forging them into a recognizable culture of ideas ultimately, not the force of arms, which would conquer much of the world. Yet, as stated, Philip was no man of letters, and his career was for himself. But briefly he ruled a Hellenic empire which was to expand in all four directions of the compass. As are all empires and nations it had a date certain when it would be extinguished. But the ideas of free inquiry into all facets of knowledge and a voice, however constrained it then might have been, in the matters and powers that governed him was nurtured by the Greek culture which emanated from its radiance. The concept of individual worth and free will was discussed and at times exalted by the Greek philosophy, although under a man such as Philip "free will" would operate under strictly defined confines. In antiquity in the matter of belief in a person's individual worth, merit, and value the Greeks likely were subordinate only to that small nation to the south, a people of strange ways, a strange moral code, and an even stranger belief in one God only, the Jews.

The glory of Greek culture was approaching its zenith, and Philip's mastery of the arts and brutalities of public affairs gave it a solid base from which to expand. Before the Hellenic ideas could travel these roads of antiquity, soldiers, many, many soldiers would of necessity need to blaze the trail. Philip was only the beginning, and now he rested in his grave. Would his successor be equal to a task that heretofore no one man had ever tried? Could he, in effect, conquer the world and bring it all closer together and into sharper focus.

ALEXANDER OF MACEDON

In the days of the ancients (and well into modern times) to be a great leader of men it was greatly to the aspirant's advantage to be a great horseman. To be a great horseman, a man required a great horse. While he was king, Philip received an endless stream of gifts, which included a sleek black horse with the name Bucephalus. He had a magnificent appearance, but the steed was proving to be worthless. No one could ride him as he was skittish and easily terrified. Apparently giving up on the animal Philip passed him off as a gift to his own twelve-year-old son. The youth observed the black horse and noticed that Bucephalus would be terrified when he saw his own shadow. He mounted him and was careful and quite adroit in keeping Bucephalus pointed in the direction of the sun. Not only that when he mounted the horse, to the catcalls and taunts of Philip and his lieutenants, all skilled horsemen, he gently stroked and spoke to the horse, and obtained the animal's trust. Philip was so impressed that legend states that he remarked to his son:

> "O my son look thee out a kingdom equal to and worthy of thyself, for Macedonia is too little for thee."

Whether this remark is pure embellishment, pure truth or somewhere in between it is legend and provides our introduction to Alexander of Macedon, better known as Alexander the Great. In any listing of the most famous and consequential figures in all history Alexander would certainly be a strong contender for the top ten. He was the son of Philip and Olympias, a Greek woman, of plentiful ambition herself. For the purposes and currents into which his life would flow his childhood and youth were well suited. He lived a rugged, physically strenuous life, but he himself was well educated in the ways of the Greeks, having perhaps their greatest philosopher, Aristotle, as his private tutor. Philip was a man of war, and Alexander showed no hesitancy in embracing the martial life. As a young teenager he was in the Macedonian Army, and by the age of eighteen was commanding a significant section of Philip's army. Although he was royalty, the king's son, Alexander never demonstrated the slightest hesitancy in leading men from the front, and his personal courage was often on display.

Alexander was blessed with two talented, gifted parents, each an individual force with whom to be reckoned. With these blessings came an attribute which both propelled him to seek worlds to conquer but which hampered him as a man. Philip's ambitions have been chronicled, but Olympias deserves more than a modicum of attention.

She taught her son Alexander that he was descended from the deities themselves and was thus a god in the form of a man. Increasingly, Alexander's abbreviated life demonstrated that he believed this. Yes, he was gifted, but we have no need to exaggeration. As a general and conqueror, he was consummately skillful, and the Macedonian-Greek forces suffered not a whit of diminution when their command passed from Philip to Alexander. Even today the extent of his conquests remains breathtaking and non-pareil. His vision of his empire's governance and growth was an odd combination of judicious foresight and megalomania.

Alexander was a lover of the arts, of fine things and towards the end of his life began to preen himself in luxurious accommodation and finery, yet he never became decadent. Though he appreciated art, literature, and sculpture he had no particular gifts, and even discounting the moral distinctions between the two men, the shepherd boy who grew to be King David of Israel likely was his superior. What Alexander possessed in as great an abundance as any leader ever owned was a singularity of purpose, a drive for accomplishment to an end or ends, and he had the fortitude, the stamina, and the power to brook no opposition for any reason. The first days of his reign as King of Macedonia shockingly proved this.

King Philip's body had hardly commenced its decomposition when his twenty-year-old son Alexander was proclaimed, with no serious opposition, as his successor. Alexander, like all men and women who seek power, especially absolute power, was almost physically averse to the very concept of opposition. This is good because at least in the beginning Alexander had little of the friction of opposition. The logical inquiry regarding this subject is the source of the opposition, for from whence would it come. Centuries later a voice far greater than any of these men would exclaim that "... a man's foes shall be those of his own household."

For a man so generous with himself with women, i.e., seven polygamous wives and a likely larger number of mistresses, King Philip had few offspring; five, perhaps six children total. To his contemporaries and to history Alexander, his most famous progeny is a towering figure. He, too, though, was a family member and for our perusal we shall note two half-siblings, both of whom came from the marriage of Philip to Cleopatra Eurydice. Each was less than two years of age, when soon after his succession Olympias, Alexander's ambitious mothers, had both killed, ensuring that never would Alexander deal with sibling opposition to his reign. Historians differ as to Alexander's complicity in these murders, ranging from a belief in his disapproval to his full complicity, but it stretches credibility that he was unaware of his mother's criminal plans.

Before our narrative proceeds further let us offer an expanded view on Alexander the Great. Certainly, he was brilliant, in some areas almost prenaturally gifted and a man to whom many yet today are willing, even to the point of ardent enthusiasm, to accede a recognition as the greatest general and conqueror in history. Morally, though, Alexander of Macedon was a bad man – a verry, very bad man. Hopefully, we will be judicious in our usage of harsh and condemning words but rather offer historical fact to bolster this pronouncement. Before leaving the subject of Alexander's family it is well to return briefly to the murder of his father Philip. No controversy has ever existed as to Philip's actual assassin, Pausanias, the man who drove the knife into the Macedonian monarch. But did he act alone? From the day of the deed a stench of opprobrium has lingered over Alexander, and the question of his being behind his father's murder forever lingers. Viewing this question through a modern prism and employing the crime terminology of the present-day Alexander certainly possessed in abundance that trifecta deemed necessary for a murder, means, motive and opportunity.

Before he started his campaign of a dozen years to conquer as much of the world as possible Alexander had to attend to the matter of Thebes, which after Athens and Sparta was the third most important city in Greek history. Even after those two titans of the Greeks had been subdued by Macedonia, Thebes, a city to the northwest of Athens continued to provide virulent opposition to Alexander, and unbeknownst to the Thebans provided him with the opportunity to make an "example." Alexander's forces marched on Thebes, and after a five-day siege the Thebans gave way. The Macedonians broke through the city's walls, sacked the city, and killed, looted, plundered, and raped at will until thousands were butchered and at least 30,000 survivors were sold into slavery. The city was razed to the ground, and leniency shown only to the descendants of the great poet Pindar, a man known to have praised the King of Macedon. Historians have long commented that in ancient warfare such bloodshed was inevitable to a besieged city that resisted a superior force. This was true, but many things in life are inevitable, but inevitability never has justified wrong and sin. But Alexander had his "example" and any man, woman or state who dared to oppose him could expect the same retribution.

A bit more consolidation remained on the borders of Greece, but these were comparatively minor affairs. Alexander was now affixed on the goal that drove his father Philip and which was not only inherited but fully absorbed by his son, the conquest of the Persian Empire. Publicly and ostensibly, this was to be Hellenic vengeance for the wrongs, the wounds, and the battle scars which the Persians had inflicted upon the Greeks in the Greco-Persian Wars of the 490's-480's B.C. Yet this was over one hundred fifty years previous, prior to the lifetimes of the most ancient of the great-grandparents of these present Greeks and Macedonians. Undoubtedly, an element of historical vengeance was in the heart of Alexander and even most of his soldiers. Alexander was many things, but he was not a historian, so we must judge him, as we should all others said a very wise teacher four centuries hence, "... by their fruits." This never-failing standard reveals that Alexander of Macedon intended the conquest of the world.

After adding to his empire by conquests in the neighboring Balkans he turned his supremely trained forces eastward and crossed the waters at the Hellespont, entering Asia Minor. With 50,000 infantry, over 6,000 cavalry, most superbly trained, and battle hardened and led by trusted and able generals the Macedonian force was a frightening specter to any would-be foe. Already of much historical notoriety the reputation of Asia Minor would continue to grow, and Alexander would do more than his share in its construction. Little could he have known, or perhaps even cared if he had, that a few centuries hence Asia Minor would be a key battleground in another type of war, and names of the like of Paul, Barnabas, Silas, Ephesus, Tarsus and Galatia would acquire a historical fame and light even greater than Alexander's. Still, this was the future, and the present was young Alexander of Macedon and his army, often under the command of Alexander personally and when necessary, under Parmenion, his right-hand man.

Our narrative will in the main omit the details of military campaigns, battles, dates, etc. and for that matter, their outcomes. The reason for the final omission is the natural result of a realization of singularity among history's great commanders – Alexander was always successful, he always won. Except for a few minor temporary tactical setbacks, if he had been an athlete his career record would read "Retired – Undefeated." Asia Minor itself was a huge geographical bloc, and the Macedonian conquest of such a land was an invaluable springboard to the remainder of the suzerainty of the Persians.

Before plunging into the heartland of the Persian Empire, Alexander turned his army south and southwest into ancient lands, all of which had a long Biblical pedigree (certainly of no interest to the Macedonian Alexander) and with such storied names as Syria, Phoenicia, Tyre, Egypt, and Judah. He and his forces received mixed receptions, ranging from fierce military resistance in Tyre to his being welcomed as a liberator in Egypt, wherein he was proclaimed as the new Pharaoh.

Even Judah and its capital became a part of Alexander's continually expanding empire. Militarily and population-wise the Jews were quite insignificant. Alexander displaced the Persians, to whom in the 330's B.C. the Jews still owed obeisance, but it was the displacement of one acceptable ruler by another, who in the person of Alexander was even more palatable to the conquered. Whatever his moral defects, and his sins and crimes were legion, Alexander possessed certain wisdom as a ruler. As a man he had a longstanding interest in the subject to religion and proclaimed himself to be a worshipper of Zeus. As a ruler of a diverse empire of peoples and nations he tended to respect the local religious practices, so long as his rule was not challenged. To a group so identified with religion as the Jews this was a salient fact, and throughout Jewish historical recollection Alexander the Great is held in high esteem. From their history the Jews knew firsthand tyrants. They had suffered in Egypt under Pharaohs who literally saw themselves as gods, under numerous of their own kings, the grotesque Assyrian brutality and so much more. Alexander's rule was not tyranny, and if anything, it was as a liberator that he was welcomed, a not uncommon experience repeated in other lands to which he led his forces.

His empire had begun its dramatic expansion beyond the constraints of the boundaries of Greece and Macedonia, and his southern flank was secured. Alexander now turned his boundless drive, energy, and ambition to the sweetest reward of all, the defeat and downfall of the Persian King Darius III. North north-eastward Alexander led his deadly phalanxes of skilled and hardened Macedonian and Greek warriors. They arrived at Issus, located in the northeastern corner of the Mediterranean Sea, somewhat east of the more famed city of Tarsus, later the home of another of history's most famed travelers. Initially the forces faced each other across a small stream, and as usually the

Hellenic armies were heavily outnumbered by the Persians. Numbers of ancient military forces are difficult to cite with accuracy or precision, but the consensus is that Alexander commanded 30,000 to 45,000 men against a force of three to four times its size. Plus, Alexander was in a position which necessitated his going upon the offensive. The king whose realm was expanding by consistently large aggregation of lands and populations was up to the task. Alexander's brilliant tactics, his flawless execution of his plans and the skills and courage of his Macedonian troops carried the day, and the Persian army once again suffered defeat. The Persian Empire still stood, though, but the troops of King Darius III retreated deeper into Persia. At a place called either Arbela or sometimes Gaugamela Alexander's army met the Persian hordes of Darius. It was an historical juncture in time and place, and at Arbela effectively did the two-century clash between the Persians from the east and the Macedonian and Greek invaders from the west. Heavily outnumbered, as they always were in any clash with the Persians, again the westerners prevailed in yet another of history's most decisive battles.

The Persian royalty demonstrated a weird penchant to watch, from afar of course, their military forces being pummeled in battle. Just as Xerxes had perched on his royal throne on a hillside where he witnessed his massive naval defeat at Salamis, Darius and his royal retinue watched from the rear of the Persian forces. The Persian forces and with it the courage and leadership of Darius. He and his coterie of attendants scampered from the battlefield in desperate retreat with Macedonian cavalry, including Alexander himself, in pursuit. Before the Macedonians could run Darius to ground, the Persian emperor's own nobles turned upon and killed him. Alexander was now, in addition to his other honors, was now the ruler of Persia.

By this point in his Persian expedition Alexander's enemies were increasingly becoming his allies and his solders. Many of the Persians happily accepted the Macedonian's rule, and Alexander began to make the most of it. He encouraged Greco-Macedonian marriage with Persian women, and as a royal example he took the daughter of Darius, a young woman Stateira as his wife. Persian troops became a substantial portion of Alexander's army, not always without resentment by his Greek and Macedonian natives. Nothing, though, ever seemed to slake Alexander's thirst for conquest. As the previously quoted passage from the Hebrew book of Esther so denoted, Alexander gained the entire Persian Empire, all 127 provinces. Still, even that was not enough, and the exotic allure of a new Asian realm captured his attention.

Alexander pressed on into the great sub-continent of India, which most decidedly had not been part of the Persian Empire. In 327 B.C. the Macedonian began to move south from the snow-covered mountains of the Hindu Kush to a city known as Bessus. In India, as in every realm he entered and controlled new cities, invariably named Alexandria. To add to the exotica of his travels and conquests he defeated the ruler Perus, whose forces were supplemented by war elephants (a foreshadowing of a European event over a century later) at Hydaspes. Further south into India he planned to go, but now his troops, even his steadfast Macedonian brethren, said "no more" and refused to be the instrument of his endless conquest of the world. Doubtless, if Alexander could have pushed farther, and through he was enraged with his own army he knew when to back away.

Although Alexander as a general and fighter had nothing left to prove to anyone, in his latter years he began to assume less the simple role of a battlefield leader and more the life of an Oriental potentate living in the lavish lap of luxury. Still, he had plans, and the restless ambition which was Alexander would have prodded him forward. In 323 B.C. he returned to Babylon to contemplate and plan his next forays onto the world stage. Though by now proclaimed a god by most, Alexander remained a temporal, mortal human being. One evening at a drinking party he fell ill and died but ten days later. It is still hotly debated among historians whether his demise was caused by disease, perhaps malaria, by poison or by other means. In any event he perished at the shockingly young age of thirty-two.

So, what after all did the lives of this father-son duo of Philip and Alexander really mean? Undoubtedly, their lives had great effect, but that does not necessarily equate to meaning. The title to this chapter "God's Great Servants" is not self-explanatory, and our brief summary at chapter's end will by no means provide a full understanding, for that will hopefully be better developed by the ensuing chapters. Before those two kings, although the world had already seen its share of conquerors, the ancient earth was essentially tribal, with a minimum of thought beyond the clan or tribe. Philip and especially Alexander, albeit for essentially selfish and egocentric reasons, saw the world as one and began to speak in the strange terms of unity. To unify requires commonality, and again, especially with Alexander, his armies sought his personal glory but also began to spread a new outline, the Greek or Hellenic culture, wherever their armies marched. No place, no land, no nation, was ever the same after their expansion of the Hellenic world and its worldview. With the hardened, rough soldiery, and let us be honest with language the "killers" of Macedonia and Greece came a new civilization, new ways of thinking rather than merely accepting, new legal systems, the stirrings of the ideas of the worth of individuals. For so many reasons, a few just referenced, the world touched by Alexander became a different place. Let us not overlook perhaps his most practical accomplishment, the gift and dissemination of a common language, Greek, which had its greatest pinnacles in the New Testament. For that alone Philip and Alexander were the great servants of God. Like Pharaoh of old they were unwilling and unknowing, but nonetheless they were His servants.

As the young Alexander lay dying in his bed in Babylon, he was asked to whom his empire was bequeathed. To them his famous reply was "To the strongest." How shocked might Alexander the Great be if he knew that the strongest was yet to be born for over three centuries later.

CHAPTER FIVE – TO THE STRONGEST

The sixth century before Christ saw the emergence of one of the great men in the history of the Jews. Daniel, a youth taken from Judah when the Babylonians captured Jerusalem became famous under both Babylonian and later Persian rule. He is forever known as a wise minister of affairs in both empires, and of course for that perennial favorite, Daniel in the Lion's den. He excites admiration for all that he did, but no more so than as a prophet, whose Divinely guided roadmap of ancient empires composes more than half the book that bears his name. Well over two hundred years before their fruition into reality he prophesied events to come with a remarkable precision. He spoke of a figure who could only have been Alexander as:

"...a ram which had two horns,
and the two horns were high;
but one was higher than the other and the highest came up last.
I saw the ram pushing westward, and northward, and southward;
so that no beasts might stand before him,
neither was there any that could deliver out of his hand;
but he did according to his will and became great."

The funeral of Alexander was magnificent, but no more than the long procession which was to return his body to Macedonia. The coffin was placed in a carnage resembling a columned temple and covered in gold. A team of sixty-four mules (to the ancients <u>not</u> an object of derision), each bedecked with a gold crown and bell pulled the cart. One of Alexander's generals, Ptolemy I Suter, high-jacked the procession and re-routed it to Egypt, where he had established his role. And so, the conflagration to replace Alexander the Great began to rage. As for the celebrated remains of Alexander history records for centuries the notable and great paying homage. These include Julius Caesar, Cleopatra, and Augustus Caesar, but in the fourth century A.D. references cease. Before, however, the honored body of Alexander lay in its coffin, his living but expiring person received on his death bed many visitors, one of whom inquired "To whom do you leave your empire?" Supposedly, the greatest of world conquerors replied, "to the strongest." Alexander, though, was unaware that earlier God's prophet Daniel had outlined his succession. With the death of the ram, Daniel prophesied:

(W)hen he was strong the great horn was broken;
and it came up four notable ones toward the four winds of heaven."

Anyone could have foretold that with the death of Alexander his empire would fracture, and that blood would continue to flow at the commands of men determined to be his successor. Although it is speculative it may be conjectured that Alexander himself would have been hard pressed to maintain the coherence of such a large empire. His would-be successors, mostly his own generals fought and schemed until by 280 B.C. the four horns, the four successors, to Alexander had established their power over four former blocs of Alexander's realm. Their names were Cassander, who ruled Greece, Lysimachus, the ruler of Thrace and most important to our story Ptolemy I, who ruled Egypt and the Levant and Seleucus I Nicator, who ruled Mesopotamia and Persia (more precisely to the modern observer, Iran).

For the moment, though, our narrative pauses in its attention to the political events and politicians of the time. Although so many never accept this realization, no matter their fame and power all are transitory, including Alexander and his successors. More permanent are the cultural ideas, the routines, rites, rituals, and philosophies which Alexander and his soldiers brought with them. Our text has heretofore referenced "Hellenism" as the idea and culture developed by Greece, enthusiastically embraced by both Philip and Alexander, and then disseminated throughout all the lands they entered. Our references to Hellenism have, at best, been only glancing, but now the answer to the question "What was (or is) Hellenism" must be addressed.

Hellenistic, the Greeks' self-referential term for their civilization and culture, in some degree began to penetrate and permeate all lands conquered by Alexander the Great. Such a short synopsis to which we are limited is fraught with intellectual danger, for the simple reason that "Hellenism" is a word that still engenders much disagreement among wise and learned scholars. Nonetheless, of necessity for our study we will attempt to contribute a pittance worth of thought. Underlying almost all Hellenism were the ideas of individual thought and knowledge, expressed in the great philosophical inquiries, the plays of the dramatists and the innovative ideas and products of the arts and sciences. Hellenism lauded the acquisition of knowledge, a key to education and constructive accomplishment, but eventually its extreme praise and exaltation of knowledge, or "gnosis" bore (and still bears) an eerie realization of the serpent's promise in Eden, that "... ye shall be as gods."

Although Greek society had its share of the traditional honoring of its ancestors, its advancing elements fairly preached the idea that the future would not necessarily be a repetition of the past. Ancient societies were tribal, highly traditional, and at least paid lip service to ideas and glories of their ancestors. Hellenism promised more and not just more, but "new." Every era, every year, every day was the raising of the curtain on something new, nowhere more eloquently or succinctly spoken than by a physician centuries later when this man, himself a Greek but the eloquent spokesman of a truly new faith described the Greeks' brain trust:

> "For all the Athenians and strangers
> which were there spent their time in nothing else,
> but either to tell or hear some new thing."

True education and knowledge were and yet remain welcome components to a richly endowed life, but like everything else they prove to have consequences. Hellenism elevated, but to a degree, the individual, but whether intentionally or not, it altered and in extreme cases broke the traditional bonds of society, religion, and family.

The Greeks, and not a small number, moved to conquered lands, and proved to be a great proselytizing vanguard of Hellenism. Generally, it was not spread by the sword, but by example, an example that often was quite enticing to new converts. The Greek idea banked heavily on the intellect, the thoughts and world of each mind. In different terms and subject to the qualifications imposed by humans and history it encouraged each individual to think for himself or herself. In the twenty-first century AD, the logical boundaries of these Hellenistic concepts are continually being tested and their meaning questioned. Multitudes still meekly obey because the king, president, governor or mayor issues edicts or decrees, or because a priest or council of "holy" men determine one way or another.

To one degree or another Alexander brought Hellenism to every nation upon which his army, (often welcomed as liberators by those who believed themselves oppressed) marched. Every nation was touched by Hellenism and in some instances radically transformed. Once Hellenism arrived at a home it was the proverbial guest who came to dinner but never left. The concrete, the tangible, the substantive is just that, or so it seems, but most often these are the affairs of humanity that are most transient. Buildings, no matter how majestic and beautiful are razed to the ground, governments, no matter how powerful, rise and fall, and with them their rulers, whether well-intentioned or tyrannical. Nations themselves, without exception, either fall or are so radically transformed that they bear no resemblance to their former shapes. Ideas, or that word so associated with the Greeks, "philosophy" maintains a longer span of life. The Greeks were replete with philosophy and its adherents, but at the time of Hellenism's spread after Alexander's death, three basic schools of thought, all of great prominence into the New Testament world, those that came to be renown as the Cynics, Epicureans and Stoics, all terms that maintain a thoroughly functional usage in modern English. With all the Greek emphasis on classical thought and theory, strangely each of these philosophies seemed to center around practical ethics. For their adequate description and analysis at least three volumes are needed, yet our foolish boldness is demonstrated in the descriptions of a paragraph or two.

Cynicism perhaps is the philosophy that maintains the greatest modern currency. Its most famous proponent was Diogenes, who had met Alexander, and who himself renounced all earthly possessions. Live as close to nature, as simply as possible he taught, and practiced his own teachings, for he was well known for living in a barrel. He and his followers taught the superfluity of moral standards (at least as practiced by others) and preached that all men should abandon a sense of personal shame for any conduct. Except for dwelling in a barrel this philosophy remains a widespread practice in the modern world, as it did in the Hellenic.

The modern reputation of the word Epicurean comes from our imagination of the picture of a person whose culinary desires and tastes are of almost stratospheric heights. Thus, Epicurean is a gourmet who finds exquisite pleasure in the very best of food. Although this is certainly an element in the philosophy developed by a man named, unsurprisingly, Epicurus, it is not its sum and substance. Whether Epicureanism is an element of a larger philosophy of Hedonism, or rather if the reverse is true, it glories in materialisms. Epicureanism proudly projects the idea that an individual's quantum and quality of pleasure, primarily physical or temporal, is the sole measure of his life and effectively the sole standard of good. From the beginning of creation to the present it has never lacked for massive numbers of adherents, and likely never will.

Stoicism seems to be the very antithesis of Epicureanism. As a formalized philosophy it had its genesis with Zeno, an Athenian teacher of circa 300 B.C. The original Stoics lay great emphasis on nature and unfolding events, far beyond human control, as the revelation of the will of God (or more likely the gods) and proclaimed that much of man's emotional well being and happiness was tied to his ability to accept uncomplainingly things as they are. Between the Epicureans and Stoics was a natural tension that provided a backdrop for New Testament events several hundred years later.

These are brief, perhaps ludicrously truncated summaries of philosophies which the worldwide spread of Hellenism effected. Too, the immensely creative Greek mind was not limited to three philosophies so easily encapsulated in a few descriptive words. Remember, as the Biblical chronicler Luke was later to write they were constantly seeking to learn and speak of some new thing.

But enough of philosophy. Is this all that Alexander, his armies, and the ensuing colonizing elements of Hellenic (or an embryonic Western) civilization brought to heretofore lands independent and separate from Greece? Most decidedly and emphatically the answer to this question is "No." Nations, cultures and men and women do not change or even contemplate alteration in their daily lives except by force or choice of something that they believe is better. Although the Hellenistic Age had its tyrants, one of whom will be a key figure in the following chapter, the Greek ideals were not spread by tyranny. Neither were they disseminated by the musings of academics, philosophers, and want-to-be intellectuals. Cultural changes that appear attractive and offer promise of a better, a more fulfilling, a happier and, dare we say it, a more "fun" life are the catalysts for change. The Greeks brought this with them. After the roar and the effluvium of the battlefields faded and with Alexander's Macedonian and Greek forces everywhere victors, other Greeks, large numbers, began to emigrate and move into the newly won Alexandrian realms. These Hellenizing Greeks were bearing gifts, for they came not empty handed. With them came long regnant styles of thinking and living, ways of dress, wealth and for the specificity of description, a love and exaltation of learning and education. Perhaps this may best be understood by one particular Greek institution and innovation which remains inextricably limited to our image of ancient Hellenism, the gymnasium.

The gymnasium was a mainstay of traditional Greek society, and soon was introduced into the newly Hellenized lands with immense popular acceptance. The gymnasium was a school for the physical and mental training of boys and young men, and its original form it was devoted to their training for war. Increasingly, though, to both the ancients and modern Americans the gymnasium, more commonly to us, the "gym" came to be devoted to physical exercise and athletic contests. They became both common and popular almost everywhere, and even the Jewish Apocrypha recorded that:

> "They built a place of exercise at Jerusalem after the customs of the heathen."

The gymnasium was an essential element of Hellenistic life and added a large element of enjoyment that was not necessarily easy to find in ancient existence. Within its walls, the young men could exercise, swim, box, wrestle and engage in any other exercise or contest which they could devise.

A well-equipped Greek gymnasium had many rooms for the use and benefit of its students. Oiling rooms, dusting rooms, lecture rooms, and even bathrooms were part of a well-equipped gymnasium. Generally, the gymnasium was a public facility, financed by the municipality in which it was resident. The ancient world was brutal, and most persons, no matter their locale or ethnicity, lived hard lives, most hand-to-mouth, little above subsistence. The Hellenic way of thinking and life promised more, and many who had tasted it found it sweet with the promise of a happier future. In that massive geographic area that fell to Alexander, a new day had dawned which we call the Hellenistic Age. Under his four successors and their progeny, not all of them Greeks, it was a way of life embraced with enthusiasm. Everywhere Hellenism was accepted with an amazing uniformity and unanimity, and it seemed to many that Alexander truly had fashioned a world in which all men and women could find much in common. Everywhere, though, save a tiny country of little notice, minimal military value, and their own ideas of the appropriate manner of life. Actually, it was a country that held in common with Greece, more than a superficial resemblance. It was Judah.

In many fashions, not superficial either, the ancient Greek and Jewish societies could claim a certain kinship. Both prized knowledge and education, and though these assertions are impossible to quantify or prove it is probably that the Jewish literacy rate surpassed that of the Greeks. Both nations admired thinking and knowledge beyond the mundane. Perhaps, as are most generalities, it is a simplistic claim, but the Greeks sought to know themselves ("know thyself" in the famous words of Socrates), while Jewish scholars sought to know God. Both people had lengthy antecedents and deep ancestral and intellectual roots, but while the Greeks were rightly proud of their poets, statemen and philosophers the Jews proudly traced a direct ancestral path to Abraham, when God called him out of Ur of the Chaldees. The Greeks could and did boast of Pericles, Themistocles, Philip, and Alexander, but no less so did the Jews point to the vaunted Joshua and David. The Athenians especially theorized and developed systems of government, even democracy, but the people of Judah could trump this with the long extant Law of Moses.

As to the introduction of the Greek ideas and innovations in the arts and sciences a bit more of a dichotomy between the two cultures was present. The Jews', intelligent as they were, had no particular devotion to scientific and mathematic theories or practicabilities. As for the arts, sculpture, writing, dance, and others it is quite likely that most Jews saw the Hellenic developments as self-indulgent at best and immoral at worst. The Greek and classical imagery of the human body as something to be celebrated and exalted would have been abhorrent to the Jews. Further, in our brief summary and discussion of the Greek gymnasium, its exercises, and contests, omitted was a very salient fact which was obliquely referenced by a later Jewish writer in the Apochrypha:

> "They built a place of exercise at Jerusalem after the custom of the heathen."

Tersely stated, the "custom of the heathen" was that all performances and contests at the gymnasium were conducted in the nude by the participants. Raised in the strictures of the Old Testament and almost one thousand years of the Mosaical Law the Jews found this practice both opprobrious and repugnant. Nonetheless it was entirely consistent with the Hellenistic exaltation of the human, especially the human male, body.

Other distinctions between the Greeks and the Jews are notable and subject to being catalogued. It is somewhat of an oversimplification, but nonetheless the following is offered. To the intellectually aspiring Greek, a major goal was to discover more of himself, of how he should think and in what direction his development should go. The diligent, intelligent, and observant Jew focused more not on the nature of himself but rather on the nature of his gods. Glory, beauty, and knowledge, to the Jew, lay not in man or his endeavor but in man's Creator.

Although in the main the Jewish people rejected Hellenism that is not an absolute, for a degree of the new culture permeated certain branches of society. In reading and absorbing the history of the Jews' reaction to Hellenism in the third and second centuries B.C., the reader may sense that he or she is actually reviewing current events in any modern Western society. Although as a whole Hellenism made only limited inroads in Jewish society its strengths were in the nobles, much of what today would be called the upper middle class, certain elements of the priesthood and the City of Jerusalem, the only real city or urbanized area in the Judah of that day. The average Jew, which meant the farmer, the shepherd, the fisherman or an artisan more consistently resisted the inroads of a Greek religion and culture upon a Jewish civilization that was far older than the Greek.

The everyday Jew worked hard, had a family, and gave at a minimum a formalized recognition and obeisance to the ancient and unique Law of Moses. The strength of his commitment and of the direction of his heart's desires, then as now, can only be determined by the Almighty. To Hellenism and its Jewish converts (we are reminded of the ancient phraseology of the "zeal of the convert") Mosaical law must have seemed dreary, stodgy, old fashioned, and not really suitable to the new Hellenistic world. Surely it and its plodding followers, of course not as mentally adept as the new Hellenistic Jews, would fade away into obscurity of historical oblivion, enthusiastically helped along by the new Hellenes. Even the Greek gods were more exciting than the presumable over demanding God of the Torah, with His endless commandments and strictures on how to live. The Greek gods, beginning with Zeus, and added to the mix Apollo, Aphrodite, Eros and so many others were exciting, alluring and perhaps even a bit risqué. How could the God of Moses compete with that?

One would be mistaken, though, to believe that Hellenism swept Jewish society save for a few rural holdouts. The opposite assertion came much closer to reality. The Jewish cultural mores and antecedents, deeper than those of any nation touched by Alexander's soldiers, generally resisted Hellenistic inroads. By this time in Jewish national history and after the long agony of Babylonian and then Persian exile at last the Jewish people in the main had abandoned paganism and idolatry. Of course, certain intellectual dilletantes readily accepted all Hellenistic thought and ways, be they good or bad, because all societies contain those who are continually seeking some "new thing." For they must part, though, Judaism held firm, amazingly so, to the torrents of changes that followed in Alexander's wake.

In just a dozen years Alexander the Great, building upon his father Philip's ideas and labors had laid the foundation for a new order, effectively a new world. High culture, more centralization of government, an ease of commerce and trade, new ideas, education, and infinitum were all important and all had their places, yet in that elusive "grand scheme" or more specifically "Divine" plan, they are mere foothills to the mountainous importance of one commodity which he and his Macedonia/Greek armies spread. It went by the odd sounding name of "Koine." The word has the sound of perhaps an unusual woodland creature or is a misdirection pronunciation of a monetary unit. Nothing of the sort, and for that matter it is more commonly seen as an adjective before the word "Greek" itself. Koine Greek is often called by other names, Alexandrine Greek, Attic Greek, Macedonian Greek, or Biblical Greek. It was common Greek, and most specifically the dialect spoken by the Macedonian soldiers. It has no intellectual or linguistic pretentions, although some of history's most beautiful phrasing has been derived from its usage. It was spoken everywhere the king's armies went, and soon became a second language to so many people, be they Egyptian, Persian, Cypris, Indian or Jewish. It was spoken by men and women of all strata of society and became a universal language over a vast geographical domain, most specifically that which we call the Biblical world. Historically, the only rival of Koine Greek would be the English spoken by the British and later American travelers, sailors and soldiers spread by the nineteenth ad twentieth century travels. Of the greatest importance it united nations in practical ways of communication, and even spread throughout the later Roman world. No amount of emphasis is excessive when we recognize that the entirety of the New Testament was written in Koine Greek. It became the language spoken by Peter, James, John, Paul, Apollos, and others, and it became the bearer of salvation in Christ. A man of who King Philip and Alexander the Great never heard or even imagine benefited from their vast prideful conquests. Both these Macedonian soldiers, brilliant though hardened men, were God's great servants, and they unknowingly provided the circulatory system through which the life-giving blood of the son of God would flow.

Still, before any of this could fully come to pass, the political situation for the Jews was altered. In 198 B.C. this tiny province passed from the Ptolemies to a dynasty known as the Seleucids. Serious dread now appeared, and it was a darkly serious question of whether that distant ship of our Preface would ever reach port.

CHAPTER SIX – THE DESTROYER OF GOD

As we have seen, with Alexander's death in 323 B.C. came an eventual division of his massive empire into three great blocs, only the westernmost two of which we will consider for our study. Those were the Ptolemaic, centered in Egypt and the Seleucid Empire to the east. It would be a gross untruth to assert that these two remaining empires were especially peaceful and that they lived in continual harmony with each other. We will omit the wars and skirmishes, the jealousies and changes of rulers and observe the remarkable truth that they remained basically intact for the hundred years following the demise of Alexander the Great. The logical assumption was that such vast masses of land, with differing cultures and a plentitude of ambitious politicians would quickly disintegrate and splinter into an infinite number of pieces. Apparently, forces, whether human or Divine, held them together for over a century. Nothing in this world, though, is more transient and temporal than dynasties, monarchies, and nations.

Within the Seleucid Empire arose a young ruler eventually taking to himself the name of Antiochus III the Great (241-187 B.C.) who assumed governance at the tender age of nineteen. He was Greek to the core and though aggressive military campaigning expanded the Seleucid Empire until it threatened the Ptolemaic Empire of Egypt. By now a new and ultimately greater power than any previous empire was rising in the west, Rome, and to the Romans an encroachment into Egypt was too close to their home territory. Antiochus saw himself as the Greek champion against the rise of the Roman Republic but could never really best them on the field of battle. During his reign, though, the control of the obscure southern province of Judah fell into his grasping hands. The Jews then became the subjects of the Seleucids and not the Empire of the Ptolemies. Upon the assassination of Antiochus in 187 B.C. the Jews had already been servants of the Seleucids for some eleven years. During this tenure they paid tribute and gave obeisance to the Seleucids rather than Ptolemies, but the everyday lives of the Jews appeared to be unaltered. Antiochus continued the traditional Ptolemaic practice of religious toleration, so the Jews were able to continue the practice of their strange worship of one God only.

As a king, Antiochus was a good ruler and was succeeded by his son Seleucus, who himself was assassinated (how true he was when Shakespeare remarked that "uneasy lies the head that wears the crown"). He was succeeded, not without contention, by another of the sons of Antiochus III, a young man known as Mithridates, but who took upon himself the royal name of Antiochus IV, or Antiochus Epiphanes. Among his subjects and contemporaries, the new king began to be accorded the name Antiochus IV Epimandes, or literally "Antiochus the madman," and truly he did not lack fidelity to that moniker. The new king (and for clarity's sake he will be referenced as Epiphanes) was young, talented, and urbane. Let the narrative be clear and plain, though. Antiochus IV Epiphanes is history's least known great villain. He is known by observant Jews familiar with their own history and scholars of the ancient times, but to history as a whole his life has been relegated to a backwater. God, though, knew of the coming of this tyrant, and hundreds of years before his arrival the prophet Daniel prophesied of the coming of this "little horn," who:

> "... waxed great, even to the host of heaven;
> and it cast down some of the host and of the stars to the ground,
> and stamped upon them.
>
> Yes, he magnified himself even to the prince of the host,
> and by him the daily sacrifice was taken away,
> and the place of his sanctuary was cast down."

The number of martyrs to the faith which he created is small compared to the insane compulsion of more infamous tyrants, but Epiphanes is the "devil that deserves his due." Almost two thousand years later the great French thinker Blaise Pascal offered the thought that most of humanity's problems stem from the inability of someone to sit quietly alone in a room by himself. By this observation, Epiphanes was monstrously worse. He already had one empire, the Seleucid, and he wanted another, the Egypt of the Ptolemies. The Apocryphal book of I Maccabees, from which most of the next part of our story is drawn observed that:

> "Now when the kingdom was established before Antiochus (i.e. Epiphanes),
> he sought to reign over Egypt, that he might have the dominion of two realms."

In other words, if one empire is good, two is better.

The self-confidence of Epiphanes was certainly enhanced, and his reputation burnished by his first foray into Egypt in 170 B.C. His army marched into the land and captured all of Egypt with the exception of the great city of Alexandria. The Land of the Pharaohs and for so long the Land of the Ptolemies was now under the ruling thumb of Epiphanes. Likely, for the sake of show and his own convenience he retained Ptolemy VI as the puppet-king of Egypt, but all knew who pulled the puppet's strings.

In all this where was Rome? The rising western republic always zealously protected its frontiers and buffer states and would have been expected to resist this Seleucid incursion. Fortunately for Epiphanes Rome, whose power was rising but was not yet of the gargantuan proportions it would become, was already heavily committed to another major war known as the Third Macedonian War. Egypt, and a reckoning with the upstart Antiochus IV Epiphanes would be postponed until a later day, a day that would soon come.

Following his great Egyptian victory in 170 B.C. Epiphanes and likely most informed observers viewed himself as the coming man in the power politics of the time. He had returned home, consolidated his power and empire, but in those portentous words of the Apochrypha he wanted, and for a man such as Epiphanes, he needed more. Thus, a return to Egypt was in the offing, and this time the great city of Alexandria would fall to his forces, thus effectively obliterating the Ptolemaic Empire from history. He would remain standing, and one hundred fifty years later Alexander the Great would have his true successor as master of the world. Not just Egypt, but Epiphanes planned the capture of the large, important Mediterranean island of Cyprus. His assumed successes would move him close to the doorstep of Rome itself.

It was 168 B.C., and the fine large battle tested armies of Seleucid soldiers moved into Egypt in their long trek across desert sands. Antiochus IV Epiphanes, already an immensely powerful man, most certainly and with great reason was imagining himself as the coming man, the greatest figure in the ancient world. Forward he led his army until but three miles from Alexandria itself the solitary figure of a man appeared in the distance. This one man seemingly was all that stood between Epiphanes and the prized plum of Alexandria. With a certainty he must have appeared a strange and perhaps even a serio-comic figure as Epiphanes and his massive forces approached. He was soon identified as Gaius Popillius Laeman (Popillius to history), and he was the Roman envoy in Alexandria. Popillius was an older man and of no apparent physical prominence. When word reached Epiphanes, the great leader was excited to meet a high official of Rome itself. With cordiality, friendship and perhaps even a bit of bonhomie Epiphanes strode forth to greet and welcome the Roman ambassador. His hand of friendship, though, went unaccepted and instead Popillius handed Epiphanes a document on which the famed letters SPQR boldly appeared. In Latin it stood for the phrase "senatus populusque Romanus" or in English "the senate and people of Rome." It was a certification which appeared on official Roman documents, on public buildings and even on flags and banners. The letters SPQR were meant to focus the reader's attention and sobriety of thought on their seriousness. Attention grabbing as they were, though, they were secondary in importance to the message which they certified and emphasized. The blunt epistle was a command from Rome to Antiochus IV Epiphanes that he withdraw all his forces from Egypt and Cyprus. This was from the earth's most powerful entity, a republic that had just emerged victorious from the Third Macedonian War and not long before had pummeled the Carthaginians and their legendary general Hannibal in the Punic Wars. As Epiphanes read and absorbed this message the old veteran Popillius, in a dramatic flair worthy of an Old Testament prophet or the greatest dramatist Shakespeare, unsheathed his sword, and walking in a circle around Epiphanes enclosed him by a line in the sand.

The written message had also included, depending upon one's historical inclinations, a promise, or a threat, that if Epiphanes did not withdraw, he would be at war with Rome. Popillius, looking at Epiphanes, and likely viewing the countenance of a man struggling with a potpourri of emotions, shock, dismay, and fear, added to the Roman written message:

"Before you withdraw from this circle
give me an answer which I can take to the senate of Rome."

Antiochus IV Epiphanes, ruler of the Seleucid Empire, was daring, brash, resourceful, and spectacularly accomplishing in attaining his goals. He, however, was not an impetuously rash fool because he knew that his power could not, at least for now, challenge Rome. Thus, he told Popillius that he would withdraw. Rarely has any man, much less a powerful ruler, suffered humiliation to match that of Epiphanes. He stood there on the desert sands, a proud ruler and proud general of a potent army and the ruler of a great expanding empire. Now, in but a few moments, it had all changed. As the sun beat down and in front of his entire army, his generals, his attendants and his servants, Epiphanes became as meek as a mouse, and in the plainest of language, he showed the white feather, turned tail, and ran for cover back home (but not before shaking the hand of Popillius which he offered to the humiliated king).

The emotions and feelings of any person are hard to conjecture and delineate with any certainty, and ruling monarchs of over two millennia past can be difficult indeed. Certain modern historians have asserted that Epiphanes was actually relieved by this rebuff from Rome, inasmuch as he now had the excuse not to continue with a war in which his victory was doubtful. Without doubt those views have been expressed by contemporary historians with knowledge and impeccable academic pedigree. Nonetheless, they veer into the realm of the nonsensical. He was a man, an extremely prideful man with predatory ambitions and had become accustomed to victories. The idea that he would organize giant military and naval forces, with all the effort and expense that entailed, and then be secretly happy that they were rebuffed while he was publicly humiliated is prosperous. Antiochus IV Epiphanes, the reigning monarch of the Seleucid Empire, had been cowed into submission, denied glory, and disciplined as a petulant overreaching child. Mightily had he paid for his hubristic desires for more glory and grandeur. Unfortunately, a powerful king has the means to make many others suffer and pay extraordinarily, and to those ends Epiphanes now directed his attention.

HELL COMES TO JUDEA

For the moment we interpose a twentieth century figure, that most infamous of historical villains, into our look at the pre-Advent history of the Jews. One of the world's few individuals, who literally needs no introduction, Adolf Hitler, left the world a primer for his planned conquests and the destruction of the Jewish people within the pages of <u>Mein Kampf</u>, written before his rise to power. Although he never followed his own writings with specificity this early warped autobiography draws a general outline for what became the twentieth century Holocaust and Hitler's own personal reasons for his most extreme anti-Semitism. Unfortunately, we have no written grand design for what was effectively the first Jewish Holocaust of the 160's B.C., but the author of the persecution itself was our subject, Antiochus IV Epiphanes. For two millennia, though, scholars and theologians have studied, debated, and conjectured over the rationale which drove Epiphanes to a campaign of Jewish persecution which, if left unchecked, would have destroyed the Jewish people, their culture and to Epiphanes, even their God. We will briefly note but a few but offer an opinion that none is fanciful and that all have a certain logic, coherence and verisimilitude which should be respected.

The king who returned from his Egyptian foray was a humiliated man and a humiliated king. He had gone to join the ranks of the ancient superpowers, had been rebuffed and had slipped back home with self-esteem low and inner rage and fury high. To men such as Epiphanes the woes that beset them, their troubles, and difficulties, one never to be traced to their own mistakes and fallible thinking and actions. Somebody, sometimes "anybody" is selected as the scapegoat to bear the rages of the great king. From their religion the Jews certainly knew about the "scapegoat" and later it became a term of recognition for the murdered Jewish people in the horrors and conflagrations of the 1900's. The Jews, after all were weak, relatively few in numbers, had no recent martial history, were already under the domination of the Seleucids and were thus a logical victim for the rage of Epiphanes. Besides, no one, least of all the Jews, could or ever would deny that they were different from other ethnicities.

Unlike everyone else in the Seleucid Empire the Jews, save for some grudging acknowledgements by a distinct minority of their number, had rejected the supposed modernizing and civilizing patina of Hellenism. These strange Semites clung to old notions of one God only, fanciful tales of great deliverers, promises of even greater redemption and the stodgy old Law of Moses. The desires of the powerful, the would-be powerful and their various acolytes to make everyone and everything conform and be uniform should never be underestimated. Since we have already indulged in one twentieth century reference to the totalitarian regime of the Nazis, we ask the reader's indulgence as we cite another. Hitler's number two man for many years was Hermann Goering, alternately sharp-witted and a comical buffoon but a man who once expressed his desire to see "... all Germany uniformed and marching in columns." No dictator, despot, totalitarian regime, and no overreaching administrative system of any kind will tolerate diversity and differences. Uniform, look alike, think alike, act alike, are all easier to control than independent people whose ultimate allegiance is not to the state but to God. Doubtless this was what Epiphanes saw in these recalcitrant, rebellious Jews. They would either conform totally and absolutely to the Seleucid Hellenistic pattern, as defined by Epiphanes, or they would be exterminated, and exterminated in the literal sense. God's Chosen and even their God Himself would be destroyed and eradicated.

Persecution and genocide certainly are never justified, however, it may to some degree be explainable. The Jews, or at least some of them, gave Epiphanes an initial justification (or, better stated, a rationalization for action). As usual, various individuals and sects were disputatious with one another and were contending for place and position. A Jew named Jason had become High Priest, the single most important religions and political position among the Jews. He had secured his office by an age-old custom; in that he had given Epiphanes a bribe. Jason could not maintain his perch indefinitely, and a fellow Jew named Menelaus, a Benjaminite (priests were required to be Levites) deposed Jason. When Epiphanes was in Egypt his death was rumored. Jason then led an army of over a thousand men to retake both the high priesthood, a religious position, and the temple itself. When the humbled and humiliated Epiphanes returned from Egypt he was informed of these events and was swift to act. Epiphanes now had his rationale, his outlet for rage, after his historic humiliation by Popillius, an old man, yet an old man had wielded the power of Rome. Again, we rely upon the Apochryphal book of II Maccabees, the textual basis for much of the next section of our story:

> "When these happenings were reported to the king,
> he thought that Judea was in revolt.
> Raging like a wild animal,
> he set out from Egypt and took Jerusalem by storm.
> He ordered his soldiers to cut down without mercy
> those whom they met
> and to slay those who took refuge in their houses.
> There was a massacre of young and old,
> a killing of women and children,
> a slaughter of virgins and infants.
> In the space of three days,
> eighty thousand were lost,

> forty thousand meeting a violent death,
> and the same number being sold into slavery."

Epiphanes was off to an impressively rousing start with 40,000 corpses and an equal number condemned to the degradation of slavery. It has become cliched to refer to a man such as Antiochus IV as a madman or an insane maniac. Perhaps, but we shall leave it to the historical psychiatrist to issue such a diagnosis. Our Apochryphal writer, though, succinctly but thoroughly informs that Antiochus left Egypt in:

> "... a ferocious mind...
> And commanded the men of war not to spare such as they met,
> and to slay such as went up upon the houses.
>
> Thus there was killing of young and old,
> making of men, women and children,
> slaying of virgins and infants."

Still, Epiphanes was not content, and his conduct bespeaks not just political expediency but of an inner, psychological need of destruction of the Jewish people and their culture, to whom he had consciously or unconsciously transposed all his woes and difficulties. A term of both Biblical and historical currency fits perfectly. In the Jews he found a "scapegoat" to suffer punishment for his thwarted ambitions while in the same moment he discovered the opportunity to rid himself of this unpleasant, pleasant, and undesirable people. They would either conform without fail to the dictates of Epiphanes, or he would be the destroyer of both the nation and their God.

Not only was the road which Epiphanes now began to travel a bloody and destructive highway for the Jews it was totally at variance with well over a century's worth of religious toleration and freedom within the Seleucid Empire. Historical, moral, and legal restraints, though, mean nothing to the ilk of men such as Antiochus IV Epiphanes. The subjugation and/or eradication of the Jews was likely only a means to an end for Epiphanes. His real goal always was being accepted as a major player on the world stage, a man who ruled an empire that never again would fear to cross any line and back down to Rome. Whatever measures necessary, and then some, were now to be undertaken. In this era of the 160's B.C. at times it is difficult to describe events with chronological precision since they all seem to tumble upon one another. Still, a brief description of the policies and outrages of Epiphanes and the sufferings of the victimized Jews is in order.

Epiphanes, or at least his advisors and counselors, knew that by this juncture of Jewish history the heart and soul of this small nation was its religion, a quirky illogical religion that had an abundance of laws and regulations yet only one God to worship. Destroy the Jewish religion, its God and the people's loyalty and adherence to both, and the Jews themselves would be destroyed. They were a people of the Law and the Book (what we now call the Old Testament), both of which were strikingly different from anything possessed by any other nation. The Jewish worship services required the written law. Thus, for Epiphanes's designs he decreed the systematic destruction of all scriptures and the proscription of their usage in any manner. The penalty for the decree's violation, naturally was death. The Jewish religion, like most religions, is a faith with a calendar of Holy Days, of special observances, of times of feasts and various gatherings, most ordained by God Himself. All these were now to be banished.

Epiphanes, his minions, and henchmen, were sparing no one, no mater his station. Eleazar was a venerated scribe and teacher of the Law who had attained the advanced age of ninety. A "man of distinguished bearing" he was apprehended and was to be forced to eat pork, the ultimate anathema to Jewish dietary restrictions. He refused, and his age being no defense Eleazar was flogged to death for his offense.

Like all tyrants Antiochus IV Epiphanes maintained a well-developed practical, or more precisely materialistic aspect to his character and rule. The Temple of Jerusalem was the repository for various items made of silver and gold. When the Babylonians came some four centuries earlier at King Nebuchadnezzar's orders the Temple had been looted. Again, Epiphanes's directive the Seleucids absconded with the precious metals, thus bolstering the treasury of Epiphanes. At least for a time temple "worship," if it could be so dignified by the name was allowed by Epiphanes, but only at his whimsical discretion and dictates. The Seleucids heated the observant Jews to the emplacement of a graven image of the Greek god Zeus on the sacred altar itself. Zeus, the supreme, among any, deity in the Greek pantheon had this forcibly replaced the God of the Jews in their holiest sanctuary. Surely nothing could be more disgusting, humiliating, and ignoble than this act of mockery, sacrilegious jest, but not so. Epiphanes took his contempt one step forward. Just as surely such an assumption would be wrong.

Upon the decree of Epiphanes his Seleucid "priests" began to use the altar of the Temple as the centerpiece of a slaughterhouse where pigs were butchered and offered in sacrifice to the Hebrew God. Only with the greatest mental strain may the observer conjure a more sacrilegious and depraved act, yet again the Seleucids did not disappoint. The religion's ritual of circumcision, ordained by God Himself to Moses on Mount Sinai was forbidden, and its violation at pain of death. The historian Josephus records an incident wherein a young mother was apprehended and with her was her newborn baby who had been circumcised. The baby was killed, hung from the neck of the mother and she forced to walk around Jerusalem so burdened. Over two centuries the New Testament Book of Hebrews took note of the direness of the times for the faithful:

> "They were stoned, they were sawn asunder,
> were tempted, were slain with the sword;
> they wandered about in sheepskins;
> being destitute, afflicted, tormented..."

More than dramatics almost compels the observer to seriously inquire as to whether God's plans for mankind's redemption, given a human face so long before when Abraham was called from Ur of the Chaldees has reached its terminus? The Chosen are reduced to a small pocket of land inland from the eastern coast of the Mediterranean Sea. This Judea, a small area with a small population has no recent historical military tradition. It is agrarian, desperately outnumbered, contentious even within themselves and already badly damaged by Epiphanes, a bloodthirsty tyrant who is required to cede no place or position in history's rogue's gallery of his fellow butchers. He is the undisputed ruler of an impressively strong empire. He has ordained that the Jews bow the knee, submit to his whimsical tyrannies, abandon their God or... die.

The end of this strange, yet compellingly unique people is in sight. With their destruction will their even stranger "God" fall silent? In the context of our narrative is that little far-away ship from our Preface sinking into oblivion?

An answer to the above query was inchoate but began to crystallize in 167 B.C. when an emissary from Epiphanes's government came to the small Judean village of Modein and there met an old obscure Jewish priest. The priest's name was Mattathias Maccabees, and he had five sons.

CHAPTER SEVEN – THE RETURN OF JOSHUA AND DAVID

The everyday speech of men and women has always been replete with catch phrases, repetitive words, different word melodies and harmonies that each individual employs. One of the tritest of these is the "cliché" an oft-repeated idea, truism, principle, or phrase that is sometimes applicable but often forcibly wedged into conversation to make a certain point. Although writers, including historians and theologians, may be presumptively pretentious as to think they are above this unfortunately most are not. Some of the most time and usage worn cliches of historical authors is that a certain event or coalescence of happenings is a turning point in history, a watershed event, or the turning point of the tide wherein history is channeled, sometimes radically, into new directions. If history actually had as many crossroads, turning points, points of no return, and so forth as many writers offer it would indeed be a confusing maze of starts, stops, braking, reversals and routes taken and not taken. Our collective over employment of these terms and concepts has an additional drawback, in that it may tend to lessen the impact of the reality and the drama of a moment in which history does begin to change. It occurred in the small Jewish settlement of Modein, located perhaps thirty to forty miles southeast of the modern Israeli city of Tel Aviv.

The vengeful bloodlusts of Antiochus IV Epiphanes had yet to be sated. His soldiers had ravaged Jerusalem, piling up corpses by the tens of thousands and selling an equal number of what would become the living dead into the abyss of slavery. The sacred temple even to the sanctuary of its Holy of Holies had been pummeled, looted and the situs of deplorable sacrilege that would trouble the conscience of even an atheist. Women had their babies ripped from the comforting arms, slaughtered, and abused for no other reason than that were the seed of Abraham, i.e., Jewish. Further, the Temple was looted of its treasures, and now the edicts and decrees began to appear banning Jews from Practicing their own religion and living their own way of life in their own country. Under pain of death the worship of the Hebrew God was prohibited, and Jews were forced to become Hellenistic in their lives, beliefs, and practices. The psychopathic rage of Epiphanes seemed to be incapable of satisfaction, no matter how many Jews kneeled to him or how many streams of Jewish blood flowed. Before history's pages were darkened and besmirched by such hideous events at the later pogroms (persecutions) of the Jews by the Russian tsars and before the hideous spectres of Hitler and Himmler had arisen from some Satanic abyss the Jews faced the insatiable wrath of Antiochus IV Epiphanes. The first Holocaust was at hand.

The Seleucid emperor was nothing if not methodical and thorough in his plans for remaking Judea while simultaneously destroying the recalcitrant Jews and their religion. Epiphanes dispatched his officials to all the rural areas of Judea, both to confiscate land from the Jews and erect altars for sacrifice to the "new" Hellenistic gods and goddesses. At the little village of Modein such an altar was constructed, and the day arrived when the sacrificial animals were to be offered to the Greek deities. The local priest, the aged Mattathias, refused to partake in such blasphemy. Not all Jews, though, were as pure in their devotion to God, and another stepped forth to take the place of Mattathias in offering the sacrifice. The aged Mattathias, enraged at the profanation of the altar, killed his fellow Jew with the thrust of a knife and for good measure, also slew the Greek officer who had accompanied him.

Even as the blood yet dripped from the knife of Mattathias he realized that his lifespan had been reduced not just to days, but to hours. Age or not, priest or not, he was now the most wanted man in all Judea, wanted, desired only by the government of Epiphanes but also by an increasingly large and abundant Jewish population which had made peace with the Hellenizing Greeks and had gone over to their pagan practices. To even survive for a short period, which itself seemed highly doubtful, Mattathias was compelled to leave home and isolate himself in the mountainous wilderness of Judah. Not easy for anyone, but for an aging priest of newly found notoriety the task seemed problematic and the results dubious. Nonetheless, Mattathias and his family, composed of five sons and their families, along with any who wished to join them as outcasts in the new Jewish power structure and society were welcome to share a very dangerous exile. The five sons of Mattathias all bore strong traditionally Jewish names, and they were Joannan (a/k/a Caddis), Simon, Judas "who was called Maccabeus," Eleazar and Jonathan. No ages are recorded, but subsequent events seem to testify as to all five men being in the primes of their lives. At least the family, reduced to dire circumstances remained adherent one to another, solid in their familial bonds, loyal to their Jewish heritage and yet ready to serve their God. In the remainder of Judea, how bad circumstances must have appeared.

Often there is a universalism in circumstances, spirit and emotions that makes all men and women brothers and sisters and that bridges the chasms and gorges of time, place, and circumstances. Judea in the 160's B.C. was a far cry from modern Western society, but most certainly we may imagine the emotional state, the fears, anxieties, and terrors of the remaining faithful Jews. Matters were already horrible, but what old Mattathias did, had made everything worse. Surely, such a lament was in the hearts and on the lips of many Jews. So also, was that universal emotion of longing for the past, for better times, when situations did not seem as perilous, and problem ridden as the present. Even two thousand years ago the Jews had suffered a super abundance of tribulation and heartache, but now they were on the precipice, the edge of an abyss. They stood in the long, lengthening, ever darkening shadow of a despot who wanted to destroy them, a tyrant with the military and political power than equal to the task. How frequently in their hearts and in their speech must the Jews have uttered laments for the past, for better times, for the great and heroic figures of their past, now all dead and gone, who would rise again and save them. Moses, Samuel, Gideon, Samson, Elijah, Josiah endlessly those greats must have excited and tormented the mind of the Jews. Excited, yes, but those days were gone. Perhaps most relevant to the direness and darkness were two names, honored, glorious, revered names from the past, Israel's two greatest military figures, Joshua and David. With sadness and regret and frequency the names must have been recalled and lamented over and over again. Too many regrets and too many tears, though, because Joshua and David had returned. In that wilderness of Judah where Mattathias and sons had fled a new Joshua and a new David were to emerge into the spotlight of history.

The real Joshua, the great lieutenant of Moses and his successor as Israel's leader was sound and solid, a faithful man and a brilliant, experienced leader of the Jews in their conquest of Canaan. David, the shepherd boy who became king, was doubtless the most talented, brilliant, and glamorous leader in all Israel's rocky history. Let us not forget, though, that David spent a substantial portion of his life as a wanted man, a leader of other fugitives seeking to escape the wrath of a tyrannical king. Where was such a leader now, and where was there a Joshua, a great leader of a well-organized army which represented the entire nation?

Mattathias called his five sons together to speak to them in the temporary haven of the wilderness, and the old priest proceeded to give them both inspiration and a charge which few have ever received. The only means to give real justice to the words of Mattathias is to quote in its entirety Chapter Two of I Maccabees in the Apochrypha, a chapter of seventy verses. Its entire quotation is prohibited by space and proportionality, but let it be reckoned that few speeches, even including the Bible, have an emotion and inspiration as does this. Mattathias began by a summary of the depressive dilemma in which the Jewish people were ensnared. A Gentile people had come to forcibly impose their ways, customs, and worst of all their duties and version of morality upon the Jews. They had pillaged them of their wealth, enslaved and slaughtered their men, defiled, and raped their women and grotesquely profaned God Himself. He succinctly offered a summary and a query as to their present state of piteousness:

> "Behold, our sanctuary,
> even our beauty and our glory,
> is laid waste,
> and the Gentiles have profaned it.
> To what end therefore shall we live any longer?"

It is hard, extremely hard, to not only assess a bad situation soberly, but perhaps just as difficult, or more so, to verbalize the peril aloud. Mattathias was that rare leader who possessed such fortitude:

> "If we all do as our brethren have done,
> and fight not for our lives and laws against the heathen,
> they will now quickly root us out of the earth."

As few nations or ethnicities have ever confronted, the Jews were staring national death and extinction in the face. Either they could be passively subservient to Antiochus IV Epiphanes, or they could fight. Should they and the remaining Jewish people elect the former they would do for their own people what lay beyond the grasp of Pharaoh, the Philistines, the Canaanites, the Amalekites, the Assyrians, the Babylonians, and the Persians, that which lay out of the reach of all the kings, foreign and domestic, the corrupt priesthood and generation following generation of indolent, uncaring Jews. They would destroy their nation and God's plans for redemption simply by giving up, by surrendering to a tyrant and his culture of systematic blasphemy, cruelty, and paganism. Or they could assume the burden, and maybe just a bit of historical glory or at least notoriety, by "taking up arms against the foe," a battle which might in the end prove fruitless and self-destructive to them and their freedom. That rarest of rare moments had arrived, and it was temporarily resident in the camps of Mattathias, his sons, and followers that day in the Judean wilderness. Wise old Mattathias seemed to be aware that the true moment in two thousand years of Jewish history was before him. Would he, an obscure aging priest, be able to rise to the moment's call?

Old Mattathias, who knew that he had but a short time to live and but a short time in the historical saga of the Jews (a fact which doubtless would have been of no consideration to him) was equal to the moment and a worthy successor to that cloud of witnesses in Israel's gloried past, from Abraham and Moses through Joshua and David he was made of the same faith and steel of character which we still cherish in those more famous and revered heroes of faith. To the followers who joined him and his sons he recounted not just their present struggle but the long, i.e., two millennia long, struggle of the Jewish nation and people just to survive. The Apochryphal rendering in 2 Maccabees spotlights a speech with the inspirational lift and eloquence of any in the Old Testament. Mattathias summarized the genocidal, religions and cultural destruction that was Epiphanes and his brand of evangelistic Hellenism, and charged them so:

> "...my sons, be ye zealous for the law,
> and give your lives for the covenant of your fathers.
> Call to remembrance what acts our fathers did in their time."

As a traditional Jew Mattathias was quite aware of the nation's past glories, failures, and troubles, and he was particularly keen to stress the great historical lineage from which the present Jews came. He cited Abraham, Joseph, Aaron, Joshua, Caleb, David, Elijah, Shadrach, Meshach, Abednego, and Daniel, and called for his sons to extend this brilliant record of faithful service to God. Only through rebellious brutal war did Mattathias see any hope for the Jews:

> "Recompence fully the heathen and take heed as to the commandments of the law."

Within one year of self-imposed but necessary exile in the wilderness Mattathias died. Before his death, he had stepped a bit out of character for a Jewish patriarch. He had five sons, and the Jews had always placed great weight upon the eldest son in a family, weight, responsibility, authority, and respect. Mattathias praised his eldest son Simon as "... a man of counsel" and advised his family to "... give ear to him always." The days ahead, though, were to be days of war, war which demanded the skill of arms and that special, but oh-so-rare quality that allows certain men to successfully lead others into battle. For the leader in the harsh cauldron of forthcoming battle Mattathias directed all eyes to his middle son:

> "As for Judas Maccabeus,
> he hath been mighty and strong,
> even from his youth up:
> let him be your captain,
> and fight the battle of the people."

"Maccabeus" was an ancient Hebrew word meaning "the Hammer," and it was well selected and well descriptive of Judas. Soon, not only he but his brothers would be accorded the name of "the Maccabees," and historically this is still the title they bear, they and the "Maccabean Revolt" which they would soon launch.

This is now 166 B.C. and fighting and conflict would continue for several more years, yet as we in modern times tend to remember and chronicle warfare and its battles the war, most commonly to become known as the "Maccabean Revolt" was not easily surmisable in the words and jargon of standard military history. The Maccabees would continually clash with two enemies, the Seleucid forces of Epiphanes and a large section of the Hellenistic, or to some more sympathetic sources, "reform Jews." Certainly, the latter was no historical novelty because the Jewish people were historically well inured to shedding Jewish blood.

The campaign of Judas Maccabees and his followers began in earnest in 167 B.C., and from its beginnings Judas demonstrated such a knack for what is now called "guerrilla warfare" that even today he is recognized as one of history's great masters of this skill. Successful practitioners of such know that to overcome the natural, sometimes overwhelming, advantages which the enemy possesses certain dexterities and skills must be emphasized. Judas began his campaign in the countryside and in villages, circumcising the uncircumcised Jews, destroying pagan altars and idols which had been erected. His name of Hammer was well suited, not just for his ferocity towards the enemy but also for his hardness with his fellow Jews, many of which were conscripted into his forces unwillingly. Even at the onset, though, the Maccabees appeared to generate momentum and force. Early in the war Judas even emerged victorious in two battles against regular Seleucid forces, clashes known as the Ascent of Lebonah and the Battle of Berth Horon.

Although of no particular military experience the Maccabees won a major moral victory in 165 B.C. when Antiochus IV Epiphanes left this part of his empire and departed east to Babylonia. The descendants of Abraham had suffered under many regimes and despots who seem to have adopted no purpose in life other than the persecution of the Jews. In the following millennia they would suffer countless others, even countless nations, some yet to the present, dedicated to their extermination. Still, until the rise of a diabolically Satanic predator in the central Europe of the twentieth century they would see no one to match the Seleucid, Antiochus IV Epiphanes. Yet, he still lived, and his soldiers and even a considerable segment of the Jewish populace continued to wage war against the Maccabees.

The war continued unabated, but the Seleucids were never able to corner Judah and his adherents as with increasingly desperate fervor they sought his destruction. Later towards the end of 165 B.C. the Maccabees prevailed in the Battle of Emmaus and with the Seleucid leader Epiphanes having fled to Syria the tide had turned. The war was not yet over, but now not just a chimerical possibility, but a Maccabean victory loomed as an inevitability. Against an organized Seleucid army in 164 B.C. the Maccabees won the Battle of Beth Zur. With this defeat and news of the death of Antiochus IV Epiphanes the Seleucid forces retreated into Syria, leaving the field, at least for the moment, in the hands of the Maccabees. The road to Jerusalem and the Temple lay open to Jews and to Jews alone. Judah saw his golden opportunity and as an increasingly adept military commander and a Jew fervently dedicated to Judaism he spoke:

"Then said Judas and his brethren,
Behold our enemies are discomfited:
let us go up to cleanse and dedicate the sanctuary.

Upon this all the host assembled themselves together,

and went up into Mount Sion."

When they arrived at the Temple the sight to a faithful Jew was a calamitous outrage and probably best described by the original scribe:

"And when they saw the sanctuary desolate,
and the altar profaned,
and the gates burned up,
and shrubs growing in the court as in a forest,
or in one of the mountains,
and the priest's chambers pulled down;

They rent their clothes,
and made great lamentation,
and cast ashes upon their heads;

And fell down flat to the ground upon their faces,
and blew an alarm with the trumpets,
and cried toward heaven."

Indeed, the Temple, after the horrors of the Seleucids was in a pitiable and profane condition, but now the time of restoration and rebirth was at hand. Judah Maccabees was certainly not a man or a leader to accept even the most wretched conditions passively. Jerusalem still contained Seleucid and anti-Maccabean forces, which Judah ordered put to the sword. He ordered the Temple itself repaired and refurbished, and the profaned altar destroyed and rebuilt. New holy vessels, candlesticks, tables, draperies, and the like were prepared and installed. The Great Temple, around which so much of Jewish life, sometimes with a certain misplaced purpose, had revolved was made new and whole again. It was again to be the place of worship of Jehovah, the one true God. The Jewish people were both humbled and ecstatic and:

> "... fell upon their faces,
> worshipping and praising the God of heaven,
> who had given them good success."

The front of the Temple was bedecked with gold, all the gates and rooms restored and renovated and "...the reproach of the heathen was put away."

But two years previous the small nation of Judea had been backed helpless onto the edge of a great abyss of destruction, its blood shed in torrents, its women defiled, and its God spat upon, taunted, and mocked. It was a small nation, not just in the process of dying but rather in the throes of being killed. Its future was in the hands of an aged priest and his five sons. Battles still remained, but the Jews were not just surviving, but triumphing. The Temple was theirs again, re-dedicated to God, and Judah and his brothers declared a celebration for the next eight days, a memorial that was to be observed every year and still is by all practicing Jews. It is known as the Holiest time on the Jewish calendar. Popularly it is known by the word "Hannakah."

In many real and tangible ways, the Jews held more political and military power than at any point since the olden days of Kings David and Solomon. Its roots were quite shallow, and the military options available to Judah had now changed. Heretofore, for four years he had led a spectacularly successful guerilla uprising, but those days were passing. The Seleucids still possessed an army under their new king Antiochus V, an eleven-year-old boy but the de facto ruler was his Regent, a man named Lysias. This army was dispatched to Judea and joining forces with the Hellenistic Jews, temporarily besieged Jerusalem. Both sides, though, were low on food and other supplies, and Lysias was not the tyrannical despot as was Epiphanes. He agreed to revoke all anti-Jewish decrees, cease persecution, and return his army to Antioch in Syria. A strange official "peace" settled over the land, but neither the Maccabean nor the Hellenized Jews were ready to quit, thus assuring that war would continue but now in the common historical form of Jew against Jew.

The Maccabees now had to reckon with a dilemma confronted by successful military commanders of dealing with their own successes. The more battles they won, the more cities and land taken the more they were required to defend. The days of lightning like guerilla raids and incursions had faded and dwindled. Further, Judah's problems were compounded when in 162 B.C. both Lysias and Antiochus V were executed by the upstart Demetrius I Soter, who became the new Seleucid king. So, the rebellion and the killing would go forward. A period of heightened tension and indecision ensued. A man named Nicanor was appointed as the Seleucid governor of Judea and soon seemed to gather to himself both the support of the Hellenistic Jews and the undying hatred of the Maccabean Jews. Both sides clashed at the Battle of Asada in 161 B.C., where the Hellenists met with defeat and Nicanor was killed. In this war, though, the death of any individual ruler or general, no matter how skilled or important seemed to be of only faint reckoning on the course of events. Both the Seleucids and the Hellenist Jews were committed to continuing the fight, and not without success.

The Seleucid army first reasserted its authority in the north, in Galilee, where an untold number of Jews loyal to the Maccabees were slaughtered. Their army, under a man names Bacchides continued its move to the south, and many of the cities of Judea were again lost to the Maccabees. Judah, in order to maintain both personal prestige and life for his cause decided to meet the Seleucids in open battle at a place called Elasa. Here, death in battle found Judas Maccabees, and the Maccabean forces fled the field. The Apochrypha is abundant in its references which prove that he, too, could be a harsh man (as are almost all who take up the sword), but he was true to the Old Faith and Law from Sinai and may rate serious consideration as the greatest guerilla leader in history. Yet, his great cause was suffering.

Beginning in 160 B.C. the Seleucids reestablished control of Jerusalem and also of most cities in Judea. The Maccabean strength, while diminished, remained extant and its center of gravity, the Judean countryside. The younger brother of Judas, Jonathan, now rose to be their new leader. Jonathan was a worthy successor to his brother Judah. He even succeeded in making a vague and tenuous agreement with the new colossus in the west, Rome, for Rome's assistance in the event of necessity's demand. Rome, though, now, then, and forever was concerned with its own growing interests and never came to the assistance of the Maccabean Jews. Nevertheless, it is worth this brief mention of the two entities, Rome and Judea, which would become the backdrop for the later unfolding greatest events in history.

The saga of the Maccabean Revolt is worthy of a great, dramatic, even a Hollywood style climatic ending, but alas it was not to be. Gradually, the Maccabeans succeeded in establishing governmental authority in the countryside. As I Maccabees recorded:

> "Thus the sword ceased from Israel,
> Jonathan settled in Michmash
> and began to judge the people,
> and destroy the godless out of Israel."

The great beneficial blessing to the Jews was that in the decade of the 150's B.C. the Seleucids fell prey to the crippling disease which had always been so common to the Jews, civil war. The Seleucids became consumed with internal struggles, and likely from a combination of weakness and indifference relaxed their grip on Judea. Commencing in 152 B.C., Judea achieved a state of autonomy, though not complete independence yet, within the Seleucid Empire. For the first time in centuries, they assumed a mastery over their own affairs and even made a more solid alliance with Rome.

Maybe the most astonishing result of the Maccabean period in Jewish history is not necessarily political, but rather that for the first time in their existence the Chosen began to see themselves as Jews, and a corresponding burgeoning of pride in their origin, genealogy, history, law and most importantly their God, began to develop. With the continued passage of years these elements grew, and that small vessel of our Preface started to become a bit more distinct. All this will merit a more thorough conversation later, but for the present the giant looming shadow of Rome must be addressed.

CHAPTER EIGHT – THE GRANDEUR THAT WAS ROME

For the almost four millennia of history covered by the Old Testament they are not even mentioned a single time. In the Apochrypha they are referenced, but only fleetingly, yet by the time the New Testament begins it is plain from its text alone that they have become and are the dominant power in the world. They are the Romans, but really from whence did they come and who were they? Their origin has a mythology about it, but in reality, it was not especially mystical. Rome began as just another Italian village in central Italy, an inland enclave without benefit of a coastline, in approximately 755 B.C. The Roman myths proclaim that two brothers, Romulus and Remus, were rivals, and that Romulus (hence "Rome") won out, and that even now in the twenty-first century the city bears his name. Whatever the accuracy of this or any other origin story it began about this time, and as were most ancient societies it submitted to a rule of a lengthening series of kings. Yet, early Rome was never comfortable with absolute monarchy. For much of its early history Rome was subject to at least two other strong political influences. The kings themselves were elected by the people, or at least by qualified electors, so the monarchy was never an institution entirely separate from the will of the people. Secondly, and as was common in most ancient societies, certain families, or more properly "clans," had great influence. The heads of what modern sociologists would now deem as tribal organizations, could be rebuffed, or ignored only at the peril of the monarch. From these early and highly influential men can be seen the genesis of three strands in Roman history, all of which bore the fruits of enormous influence. The early family heads were the ancestors of those who would later be deemed the aristocracy, or rather in Roman terminology the "patrician" class, from which Rome drew most of its leaders for many centuries. Secondly and inextricably linked to the aristocracy was the Roman Senate, the legislative body which represented the Roman people, though the word "people" was essentially defined with aristocratic constraints. Finally, but in no way anomalous with almost all ancient societies, Rome, especially early Rome, was a prime example of that most toxic of all modern words, a "patriarchy." The paterfamilias, or male head of his family and clan, held close to absolute power over the family's members, especially in these early Republican days. Decisions regarding money, property, succession, and inheritance were all made by him. Especially pronounced in the early days of Roman history was the literal power of life and death which he held over his family. Early Rome was no paradise for women, and especially in these earlier, more rustic, and rougher times men held sway. Yet in many very real and everyday ways life was little different in any of the ancient societies contemporary with Rome. But in certain ways Rome was different.

Starting from an advantageous locale in central Italy Rome gradually expanded throughout the Italian Peninsula. As decades and even centuries passed the tiny village on the Tiber became a substantial geographical entity, and it controlled much of the Italian mainland. Sometimes other Italian territory was added by the sword, but often it was procured by negotiation and agreement. Although Rome was expansive in its earlier days it had no avaricious conqueror such as King Philip, Darius, Xerxes, Alexander, or Antiochus IV Epiphanes. Nonetheless, it usually secured what it desired, and eventually Rome and Italy became not just compatible but at most synonymous.

In these early centuries Rome had no massive standing professional army, but rather its forces boasted the famed citizen-soldiers and even inclusive of non-professional officers. Amateur, though, did not equate with incompetence, for the Romans took martial duties seriously, though not without defeats. The Romans, though, in military matters were like they were in civilian life, resilient and flexible. Their thousand-year history is replete with loss and military setbacks, but invariably they regrouped and reformed. The campaigns and battles of the Roman generals and battles as a whole have little bearing on our study of the intertestamental period. Even today they are the subjects of learned and often exceptionally well written histories, and to the interested student this vast library will be of great value. Our narrative, though, will note and discuss one military block of time, not so much for the movements of troops and the clash of armies, but rather for the character revealing aspects of the period. Fortunately, for our purposes three wars between the same two combatants fall perfectly within the middle of the period of study. Known as the Punic Wars they spanned over a century from 264 B.C. to 146 B.C. and were bloody contests to the death between the two major powers of the Mediterranean world, the Romans to the north and the Carthaginians to the south. Before the wars or even the Romans are further examined, it is necessary, profitable, and preferably interesting to become familiar with the Carthaginians.

Carthage was a city on the eastern side of Lake Tunis in what is now Tunisia in northern Africa. Carthage was a coastal city, rich from Mediterranean commerce and at its pinnacle the most important trading city of the ancient world. Like Rome northward in Europe, Carthage lay basically at the mid-point of the eastern and western Mediterranean worlds. In addition to prosperity, it boasted the greatest sailors of the Mediterranean Sea, and Carthaginian maritimus had long manned the ships of many nations. Carthage was a small enclave of land in the north African coast, with a limited population, and all in all was almost entirely dependent upon maritime commerce for survival.

Exactly who were the Carthaginians? Carthage itself was a colony founded by a people called the Phoenicians (in Latin "Punic") and had migrated from the east. Their homeland was the coastal and inland area north of Judea, which itself had once been part of their homeland. The heart of their home country was the modern nation of Lebanon. Their original name, though, is one with a distinct Biblical familiarity, the Canaanites. Those people, the traditional enemy of the Israelites, had made their power grow and expand to where they were a peril to the burgeoning might of Rome itself. When the Canaanites founded and developed Carthage, they brought with them the full panoply of their considerable skills and even more prevalent faults. They remained the same people who were the subject of God's repeated Old Testament admonitions to avoid. The Canaanites (henceforth, the Carthaginians) were pagans to the core, and the estimates of their gods and goddesses run to the thousands. None, though, to this day, was more prominent than Baal, their great deity who had been humiliated by the prophet Elijah on Mount Carmel. Moloch, another of their prominent deities, was the god to whom they still routinely offered human sacrifice. The forum of the ancient world was an almost universally cruel arena, but even here the Carthaginians routinely held their own. A Carthaginian general, heretofore a man of enormous power, could expect the supreme power of the state to fall upon him, should he lose a battle. That power took the form of the hideous punishment of crucifixion, and many historians assert that it was from these north African colonialists the Romans adopted the punishment that would literally reach its apotheosis of infamy over two centuries later.

One final mention of Carthaginian cruelty is appropriate. Whether true or not the very fact that it remains current thousands of years later reflects upon the ferocious and degraded reputation of the Carthaginians. This anecdote informs us that while preparing for a lengthy military campaign a Carthaginian general suggested that the soldiers could at least partially subsist upon the flesh of the army's own soldiers who had died upon the way.

Still, the Carthaginians were much more than ghoulish monsters preying upon the earth's inhabitants. Their maritime skills, even supremacy, has been noted. Of more lasting value is their primary role in developing a product that has never ceased to bear enormous importance, the alphabet. Long before the Greeks developed theirs and the Romans set forth the 26-letter Latin alphabet which is the literary currency of the West, the Carthaginians' ancestors had developed an alphabet, from which both Greece and Rome heavily borrowed. Further, generally the Carthaginians were diligent, attentive to necessities and capable of organizing great cities. Their naval prowess, as well, should never pass unnoticed. Well led, with adequate resources Carthage was a formidable foe for any power, even Rome. Three struggles spanning over a century would determine the identity of the master of the ancient world. They would become so bitter and protracted that their effects, which lingered for generations, were the ancient equivalent to the modern World Wars I and II. They were the Punic Wars, and ultimately, they revealed more of the Roman character and its effects upon the intertestamental world than would be believed possible.

THE PUNIC WARS

Even the name has a certain dry, even desiccated sound to it, and many have noticed this. Should a speaker wish to reference a remote event from the supposedly dark past to illustrate boredom and irrelevance the Punic Wars apparently is as good a choice as any. It is hoped that this brief narrative adds little to the boredom but rather a touch of understanding of Roman character.

By 264 B.C. most of the Italian peninsular had either been absorbed by Rome or was in alliance of some sort with the great city. Effectively, Rome controlled the mainland, and to the southwest on the African coast was Carthage, pointing directly at Italy; however, between the two powers is the large island of Sicily, which each coveted. Carthage, already controlling some Sicilian cities sought more, but if Rome was to stop the Carthaginians it needed naval strength which it had never possessed. In an early demonstration of the flexibility and innovation which would for centuries characterize Rome, it constructed its own fleet. This fleet overcame the Carthaginian mastery of the sea in 262 B.C., whereupon Rome transported an army across the Mediterranean to combat the Carthaginians on their home ground. For once, the Romans pushed too hard and too fast, with the greater part of its fleet being destroyed by storms. Rather than surrender, sue for peace or withdraw Rome offered history an insight into why it remains one of the world's most storied civilizations. The Romans built another fleet and again defeated Carthage in 242 B.C., additional proof that this Phoenician colony perhaps was not the ruler of the waves all presumed it to be. In 241 B.C. peace was obtained, and Rome obtained all of Sicily, which for better or worse, remains a part of Italy to this day. Carthage received an early lesson from Rome in resilience, flexibility, innovation and above all the Roman character of not succumbing to panic in dire situations, a trait which would be writ large in the Second Punic War.

<u>HANNIBAL</u>

The Carthaginians had uneasily agreed to a peace settlement with Rome to end the First Punic War, yet they were far from pacified. In the aftermath of the first conflict gradually Carthage increasingly under control of the Barca family, the present patriarch of which was a man named Hamilcar. This man, a general himself in the First War had two famous sons, both generals, with the strikingly Carthaginian names of Hasdrubal and Hannibal. The "bal" in each name was a tribute to the Canaanite god Baal, the deity of Jezebel and Mount Carmel infamy in the Old Testament and still high in the Carthaginian firmament of gods.

Carthage, which had lost considerable wealth and manpower from the First War turned to the west and specifically to Spain to recoup its losses. At first under Hasdrubal and then under Hannibal the Carthaginians made serious inroads into Spain, and the still young Hannibal began to gather fame and laurels to himself. From this point forward the names of Rome and Hannibal would be welded together forever. The latter phrase has a certain arresting strangeness when we consider that Hannibal was a foreigner to Rome and the greatest committed enemy the great city on the Tiber would ever fight. That assertion, though, is natural when we consider that as a small boy Hannibal's father, Hamilcar, had pledged his young some to "eternal hostility" to all things Roman. The aura and magic of the name Hannibal, even over two millennia later, has yet to dissipate, much less vanish. The story of the Second Punic War is in large measure the biography of this one man.

Hannibal, in 219 B.C., expected a Roman invasion of Spain and north Africa and to regain the initiative instituted a military expedition, the boldness of which still startles the observer. The Carthaginian leader gathered an army of tens of thousands of men, of which Carthaginians themselves may have been in the minority. His ranks included large numbers of fellow north Africans from various tribes, Spaniards from the Iberian Peninsula, Gauls from western Europe and later even Italians and Cisalpine Gauls from the north of Italy. From north Africa he planned an end run around the Romans. His polyglot army would march across Spain, southern Gaul and into South-central Europe where there it would confront the mighty obstacle of the Alps. This force, composed almost substantially of men from sub-tropical climates would cross the snow-covered Alpine peaks and finally arrive in northern Italy. And, yes, his army would be accompanied by the famous and storied corps of war elephants. Their number was never large, perhaps a few dozen at the most, many of which perished along the way. The European Romans, though, would confront upon the battlefield a foe, the size and aspect of which were unknown to them. With the implementation of logistical skills and leadership qualities of the level of genius Hannibal and his army arrived in northern Italy in 218 B.C.

In these ancient days of the Republic the standard Roman army was titled a "consular army," after the consuls, the executives who ruled Rome and were then given command of its armies. They were comprised of some fulltime professional soldiers, but basically, they were a militia force of small farmers, artisans and craftsmen called to duty in times of crisis and peril. This was all irrelevant to the skills of Hannibal and the fighting skills of his men. No matter the identity of the Roman general, the courage and tenacity of his troops or the skill of his officers, none was a match for Hannibal. In a series of campaigns and battles in northern and central Italy in 218 and 271 B.C., the Carthaginians defeated one Roman army after another. Hannibal then moved his army to southern Italy in an effort, among other purposes, to further destroy Rome by weakening and then breaking the bonds between the great city and its Italian allies.

At this time Rome never even considered what many, if not most, powers, ancient or modern, would have done, and open peace negotiations. Instead, it appointed a new commander and a dictator named Quinton Fabius Maximus, whose name, or at least its variation as "Fabian" lives yet today. Fabius was a different type of commander, for at this point he had no confidence that he could defeat Hannibal in a straight battlefield showdown. Instead, he used his army for pinprick attacks, delaying tactics that lowered the risks for head-on engagements, strategies and tactics which even today are referred to as

Fabian. Still, none of this could defeat Hannibal and Rome waited yet for that moment to come.

Meanwhile the Romans sought with some success to weaken the Carthaginians by attacking them in Spain. Still, though, the victory remained to be won, and Rome had to win it in Italy against Hannibal himself. The Romans had reason to hope and believe that Hannibal's day of reckoning had finally come in 216 B.C. near a small village in southern Italy named Cannae. Here two Roman consular armies under the brand-new consuls named I. Aemilius Paulus and C. Terentius Varruo were planning to come together to crush the Carthaginian invader. Their ideas and plans were far from foolhardy, and all seemed to be in the Romans' favor. After years of battle in a foreign country Hannibal's forces were seriously reduced in number, perhaps only as many as 40,000 infantries. Of these soldiers it is likely that only a minority were Carthaginian, the remainder being Libyans, Spaniards, Celts, even Italians who had crossed over to Hannibal. The Romans were in their own country, and Hannibal seemed to be trapped, with a river to his left and high ground to his right. Thus, the Battle of Cannae had been readied for a few hours action one August day in 216 B.C. At first the center of the Carthaginian forces gave way, and the advancing Romans appeared ready to break through the Carthaginian line at any moment. Suddenly, Carthaginian cavalry appeared on both flanks of the Roman infantry, which had been advancing into a well-prepared trap. The greater Roman force was totally surrounded, and the remainder of the day's work was nothing more than prolonged butchery as the Carthaginians slaughtered Roman soldiers estimated in the range of 30,000 to 50,000, who by nightfall were nothing more than steaming, rotting corpses. Hannibal planned and won what yet today military historians describe as the "perfect" battle, as if the word perfect is fit as an adjective for hell came to earth. Not one, but two Roman armies, had vanished in the space of one day. Rome seemingly had no army and certainly no general who could match Hannibal, who by this point was seen by the Romans as almost more divine than mortal. Battle after battle had been fought against this north African invader, all on Italian soil, close to home, and Rome was not only beaten but crushed and repeatedly humiliated. Any reasonable observer, whether in 216 B.C. or in the safe perspective offered by the twenty first century could cogently argue the case that it was time for Rome to swallow its national pride and make peace with Carthage before their impossibly gifted general could do yet more damage.

Peace, at even an exorbitantly high price, appeared as a very attractive option to Rome. Hannibal still had thousands of Roman prisoners from Cannae on his hands, and he offered to safely return them in exchange for ransom. Even without the prisoners the Roman casualties had been appalling and to most nations even fatal. It has been estimated that from ten to twenty percent of all Roman manpower now lay dead. Even the ruling body, the Senate, had lost approximately one-third of its members to Hannibal. For modern reference it is if a foreign army was marching unchecked throughout Maryland, Pennsylvania, and Virginia, all close to the capital at Washington and was bequeathing a legacy of millions of American casualties with the very real promise of adding more. Almost any government of whatever era would have acceded to the allure of peace and the promise of ridding itself of a ubiquitous foe. Not Rome, though. It is perhaps unrealistic to concede to one moment in a country's history the nomenclature of "its finest hour." Ancient Rome stood for over a millennium, and whether as a monarchy, a republic, or an empire it was a force with which to be reckoned. Today the name Rome alone conjures not just a city, a nation, or a civilization but a world. In the wake of Hannibal's offer of peace was perhaps the greatest moment in Roman history, the one through which Rome could lay claim to being a special civilization. We may rest assured that its history is overlaid with a plentiful share of the opposite. The Romans rejected Hannibal's peace offer. Not only did they reject it but also, they made definitive efforts to replenish the ranks of its army. The age of enlistment was lowered and the property qualifications necessary for military service were lowered as well. Rome was here to stay, and the courage and steadfastness present throughout all societal strata cannot easily be denied. From Rome the ancients would learn to expect many qualities, some bursting with evil, but they would also learn that once set upon a course Rome was a determined, often implacable foe.

The preternaturally talented Hannibal remained in Italy, but his strength was gradually diminishing. Gradually Rome's strength and natural advantages became more important as Hannibal was unable to obtain reinforcements from either Spain or Macedonia, which had become his ally. Also, a young Roman general, whose reputation does not blush from comparison to Hannibal. His name was Publius Cornelius Scipio, who became consul and finally administered a defeat to Hannibal in 203 B.C., which forced the Carthaginians back to north Africa. The two powers signed an armistice, but once returned Hannibal quickly violated the peace.

Finally, the two great generals, Hannibal and Scipio, met in battle at Zama in north Africa, and the Carthaginians, ending at last the most famous of the Punic Wars. The terms for Carthage were harsh, with its renouncing all territorial claims except for the city of Carthage and surrounding environs. Further, Carthage was forced to pay a giant indemnity to Rome. The sun had set on Carthage's day as a great power in the ancient world, while the blazing firmament which bathed Rome in glory and grandeur was far from its zenith. Scipio returned to Rome, was given a triumph and the cognomen of Africanus affixed to his name.

Surprisingly, perhaps even shockingly, a third Punic War remained in the offing. With sound historical reasoning and fears many in Rome did not trust the safety of the city so long as Carthage retained any viability.

CARTHAGO DELENDA EST

After the Second Punic War one of the rising stars in the Roman political firmament and himself a veteran of that war was Marcus Portius Cato, a man known to history as "Cato the elder." He rose steadily through the Roman political ranks, serving a term as governor of Spain and is known to this day as a proponent of a staunch traditionalist or conservative approach to politics and culture. He abhorred Hellenistic cultural encroachments upon the "purer" Roman ways and was still not convinced that Rome's southern enemy, Carthage, had been fully pacified, even with defeats in two wars. Cato was a Senator and to this day is famed for his great oratorical ability. He would speak on many subjects, foreign and/or domestic, in the Senate, and would end every speech with the three-word benediction of "Carthago delenda est," or in English "Carthage must be destroyed." Carthage, though militarily weak, was still a serious commercial competitor of Rome, but it is difficult to see Cato's warlike commitment as anything less than revenge. Ultimately Cato and many other Romans got their way, and Rome, this time the aggressor, commenced a Third Punic War in 149 B.C., a conflict which lasted until 146 B.C., when Carthage effectively was destroyed. Such was the overwhelming power of the Romans, and the completeness of the Carthaginians collapse that through the years, generations, and centuries yet to the present grew the story that the Romans had killed or enslaved the city's population, razed, and leveled to the ground its structures and buildings and plowed under the soil all else. Then, for good measure the Romans salted the furrow they had plowed. Whether true we leave to the reader's own proclivities to believe or not, but it must be noted that this is a story which came later, there being no accounts contemporaneous with the supposed event. What is true, though, is the reputation which the Romans were acquiring. They were an industrious, practical people who lived by law, were generally, though, not always, of some reasonableness when dealing with non-Romans and were certainly more builders than destroyers. Still, when inflamed by emotion and unsought injuries, real or imagined, they were acquiring a reputation for vengeful ferocity which never left them.

Time and the Punic Wars had wrought notable, deep changes in Roman society and lifestyle. Not a military dictatorship the supposed solution of arms was more in the fore of Roman thinking. While still a society of small, independent thinking landowners and resistant to any form of monarchy, Rome began to increasingly seek solutions and salvation in generals and other "strong" men. Its most renown, greatest yet bloodiest centuries, still lay ahead. Rome had become sole master of the western Mediterranean, but now the center of gravity was shifting to the east, to lands famous and obscure, and none more obscure than Judea.

POST – SCRIPT

The Punic Wars were the epic event of the first half of Roman history, and the wars, their causes, strategies, and tactics remain the subjects of many histories, some excellent or even superlative. The most famous of the historians remains Titus Livius (59 B.C. – AD 7), more commonly known as Livy. He was the great historian, not only of the Punic Wars but of early Rome in general, and his accounts; covering in their original form 142 books, provide the foundation for all subsequent study. When he wrote of the Punic Wars at length, he did not utilize that as his descriptive title. Nor did he call the conflicts the War Against Carthage, the Carthaginians Wars, or the Romano Carthaginian Wars. Livy simply entitled this portion of his history as the "War Against Hannibal." Rarely has one man, a sworn enemy at that, make such a deep impression on a foreign land as Hannibal did upon Rome.

CHAPTER NINE – WARS AND RUMORS OF WARS

In the early first century AD an uncredentialed teacher from an obscure Galilean village issued these words:

"Ye shall hear of wars and rumors of wars."

Such a statement remains timeless and universal, but until the twentieth century AD it is difficult to discover a century of any greater applicability that the first century B.C., and especially for Rome, which was emerging as the world's first superpower. The Roman Republic had fought endlessly, especially in the regions to its south and west and had achieved magnificent success in converting the western Mediterranean Sea into a Roman lake. Now, partially by design and partially by necessity Rome's increasingly avaricious appetite turned eastward to storied classical realms of long-standing civilizations. Yet Rome's gaze was neither myopic nor singularly directed, for its visions and desires also turned inwards. While the first century B.C. would offer history the names of many storied figures and battles it laid bare the internal viciousness of Rome in seemingly endless wars. It is no self-embossed statement to assert that at least until very modern times the first century B.C. was the most famous (in some manner infamous) century in all history. By the end of this century Rome will have undergone a self-inflicted metamorphosis from a republic to an empire, an empire that remains as storied and studied today as any time in history. More importantly this vast political entity would be more than an aggregation of states, kingdoms, provinces etc., but the setting for the most important events and the short earthly life of the most important person since the literal Dawn of the Universe.

Yet in 100 B.C. the Romans knew none of this. What they did know was that by this date a new luminary had arisen, a general named Gaius Marius (157-86 B.C.) who already had compiled a record of massive achievement. He had won several important victories in the field, had done so with a reorganized army and himself had reached the pinnacle of politics by the unprecedented feat of being named consul of Rome for five consecutive years, 104-100 B.C. Admittedly, reorganization of an army sounds almost frightfully boring, but in this instance its importance extended for the life of Rome. No longer would military service be restricted to landowners, but Marius sought the voluntary enlistment in his ranks of the plebian, i.e., the common, class and thus began Rome's long attachment to a professional army. Marius was truly a man of immense talents, the head of state as consul and the general of the army to whom his soldiers owed their loyalty. This became rooted in Roman soil and as the generations turned into centuries Rome's army was loyal to its political and military leader and paymaster and had little residual loyalty to Rome itself.

No man or woman retains a monopoly on the playing fields of history for long, and Marius was no exception. A younger associate named Lucius Cornelius Sulla (138-78 B.C.) had challenged Marius and forced him to flee Rome. Sulla, whose venality, and cruelty can still make the reader shudder, obtained command of the army, which was deployed eastward to Pontus, the area around the Black Sea, against one of Rome's most skilled and inveterate enemies, Mithridates, in the First Mithridatic War in 88 B.C. In this eastern ruler the Romans met their most skillful and cold-blooded opponent since the days of Hannibal. Mithridates was able t o wrench the great city of Athens from Rome's grip, and he slaughtered, not in battle alone, perhaps over 80,000 Romans. In this war, though, the skillful Sulla finally bested him, whereupon Rome added to its territory. When Sulla returned to Rome, he presented to them a commodity with which they had little familiarity, dictatorship.

Legally it was time for Sulla to relinquish command of his army and return to Rome in triumph. He happily returned to Italy, not just as a hero but as a "conquering hero." With the help of younger generals of the character and caliber of Gnaeus Pompeius Maximus (hereafter "Pompey"), Marcus Licinius Crassas and several senators Sulla engaged in a ruthless civil war, was fully triumphant in 82 B.C. and then as dictator engaged in a comprehensive bloodletting of his enemies on a scale never before seen by even Rome. Daily, lists of Proscription were posted throughout the great city. These rosters of names coldly proclaimed the men and women of the city which Sulla had selected for execution. Rome, ever growing in might, wealth, and fame was becoming well instructed in the arts of civil war, dictatorship, and bloody tyranny. As the narrative will disclose the city on the Tiber never really abandoned its taste for any of these qualities. Yet, there was method in his presumed madness. Those he summarily killed invariably were the propertied classes, whose wealth was confiscated for Sulla's benefit or for a demonstration of generosity to his followers. He doubled the size of the Senate, packing this august body, whose bright power was already showing early signs of dimming, with his followers. The loyalty of his army was strengthened by the distribution of confiscated lands to his soldiers. More and more power emanated from one man, Sulla, and the bright days of the ancient Roman republic increasingly became clouded.

Shockingly, though, Sulla pulled Rome back from the brink of total republican dissolution. After instituting his measures, which in the broadest sense can be termed that most oleaginous of all political terms, "reforms" Sulla abdicated his power and the old, though highly modified, constitutional order was restored. It all came at a price, an increasingly high price. The Romans, those who were so fortunate, could still be citizens, but increasingly they became subjects. The Roman Senate flawed though it had been, with each passing generation, each strongman and finally each emperor increasingly saw its luster, reputation, and glory fade, and before the elapse of much time it became little more than an advising body. The power of Rome increasingly became embodied in men such as Sulla, hardened men who were driven by the acquisitive desires for yet more power. With Sulla's death in 78 B.C. such men readily appeared. Steadily, the study of Rome evolves to where it takes upon itself a biographical hue, as "great" men rise and fall. Institutions and culture remain vital, but neither maintains the cachet of interest which men of action create.

Much happened in the years following Sulla's death in 68 B.C., certainly inclusive of events which are pivotal to our narrative, and which will be discussed in a following chapter. For the moment, though, we focus on three men who by 60 B.C. had formed what historians still call the First Triumvirate. No man could wring from the system sufficient power to rule solely, so these three agreed, with great uneasiness, to share the coveted commodity. Two have already been introduced, the first being Pompey, Sulla's young colleague whose successful generalship had brought him great personal popularity and the well-earned nom de guerre of the "young Butcher." In 60 B.C. he was no callow youth, but at age forty-six was still in his prime. The second was Marcus Licinius Crassus, reputedly the wealthiest man in Rome, a man of high aristocracy and lasting fame as portrayed by Lawrence Olivier in the 1961 cinematic spectacle "Spartacus." Crassus maintained a steadfast reputation as an unscrupulous businessman and perhaps history's first slum lord as the contractor for vast amounts of the cheap and substandard housing that blighted the city of Rome.

The third man and at this juncture the least known of the First Triumvirate was the scion of minor Roman aristocracy but a man who even while young had demonstrated exceptional military, political and what is now called "people" skills. His name was Gaius Julius Caesar (100-44 B.C.). Early in his career he had taken upon himself the mantle of the great Marius, the reforming consul and general of the previous generation, yet simultaneously he maintained the image as a man of the people. Still, he had both feet firmly planted in the dangerous yet necessary realms of Roman nobility and power. His rise to prominence was no great surprise to anyone who knew him and his seemingly undrainable reservoir of talents.

All three were men of substance and accomplishment, all were Roman to the core, and each had an insatiable drive for power that was unlikely to be fully assuaged by being one-third of a ruling committee. Such arrangements are by their very nature compromises and carry an almost inherent temporary nature. Public expressions of brotherhood among the three rulers were part of the political landscape and the Roman tableaux, yet the three men fooled not each other, and it was unlikely that they fooled the masses of Rome. The driving engine for each man was not the spirit of collegial compromise for the betterment of Rome, but rather disguised, at times very flimsily disguised, naked ambition for sole ruling power. The next few years would provide answers to the natural questions of who, how and whether would be the one triumvir who would rise to supreme power.

Crassus, the oldest of the three triumvirs, was an old, experienced hand in high Roman politics, and he certainly had no aversion to killing, especially slaying massive numbers of human beings in any given outing. Originally one of Sulla's lieutenants much of fabled wealth had come from the Sullan proscription, i.e., state sponsored murders of fabulously wealthy Romans, of whose properties he had received abundant portions. His extinguishing of the slave revolt led by Spartacus in 72-71 B.C. exceeded in ferocity and bloodshed the wildest imaginations of the producers of modern movies. To employ a weak pun Crassus was the very essence of a morally crass man, an inveterate power seeker whose penchant for bloodshed was only exceeded by his drive for power. This Roman plutocrat boasted the greatest of wealth and power of an enviably high degree, yet he was to be the first of the three great triumvirs to meet his demise. Military laurels and glory, even in our supposedly more pacified modern states, has always seemed a short, but at times enviably rewarding path to fame, glory and power. In 53 B.C. such a route opened for Crassus.

In the 50's B.C. Rome was at war with a smaller but still powerful eastern nation called Parthia. Due to Pompey's efforts in the 60's B.C. the reach of Rome had greatly expanded into the east, but Parthia remained a holdout. Military victory over the Parthians doubtlessly would reward its author in an abundant cornucopia of prestige, fame, wealth, and power. Crassus received the military command for such an assignment and to the province of Syria he traveled, where he expected to meet the Parthians in battle, achieve fame, more wealth, the plaudits of all Rome and perhaps even absolute power. Pity Crassus, though, for his hopes and dreams had been misplaced. Instead, the Roman army met a crushing defeat at the hands of the Parthians in 53 B.C. in a place called Carrhae. Evidently, a trained army was a tougher opponent than the slave multitudes of Spartacus. Not only did Crassus suffer his defeat but he lost his life at Carrhae when the Parthians murdered him in their post battle celebrations. While the Parthian King was attending the wedding celebrations for his son a courier arrived from the field at Carrhae and presented the elated king with the severed head and hand of the great Cassius. Once again, sic transit gloria.

So much more may be said of Pompey, who by the onset of the First Triumvirate in 60 B.C. was undeniably the most famous and accomplished of the three triumvirs. He had recently completed years long military campaigns in the east, the most spectacular to-date in Rome's history, had come back to a spectacular staged triumph and was the brightest star in the Roman firmament. Since some of those military campaigns were directed towards a nation of even greater importance to our story than Rome, we will defer their discussion to Chapter Eleven. Still in spite of all Pompey had powerful enemies, many concentrated in the Senate, which refused to accede to the customary land grants to Pompey's victorious troops. This was the man who essentially made the bulk of what would become the eastern Roman Empire, and yet he was being rebuffed by politicians who could boast little real accomplishment. It would be somewhat of a misnomer to assert that Pompey was not at the height of his fame, the pinnacle of his power. "Pinnacle" describes a point, but Pompey's power was so much more than that. It was a force which plateaued for many years, and as history will demonstrate Pompey gradually reconciled with many hitherto isocitrate enemies, and he became the famed colossal figure around whom so many of the traditional and conservative (not here used in any modern political sense) elements of Roman society began to congeal.

Even before his meteoric rise to fame and lasting historical glory the life of Julius Caesar had become connected to those of Crassus and Pompey. Born in 100 B.C. Caesar's father was an aspiring politician who never achieved a Roman consulship, which was his goal. Extremely intelligent young Caesar sought to widen his knowledge by studying under the famed Greek rhetorician, but on his way to study he was kidnapped and held for ransom on the Island of Rhodes. The pirates who caught Caesar soon released him, and he, no man ever to be trifled with, caught them, and had them crucified.

Caesar's first wife Cordelia died, and the ever-climbing young star married into the family of Pompey, thus, as has always been common, hoping to cement a political relationship by personal bonds. In 61 B.C. Caesar divorced his wife, a woman named Pompeia, and now he was not a part of Pompey's family.

What Caesar now became, though, was the governorship of Iberian, Cisalpine Gaul (northern Italy) and southern Gaul (southern

France). He had a brief but successful military campaign in Spain immediately before this appointment, and the prestige he had won was putting Caesar very high in the rarified atmosphere of Roman politics. Caesar had been granted the governorship of Spain, and there he had successfully bolstered his limited military experience and expanded Rome's reach and cultural influence into the Iberian Peninsula. His reputation had been burnished, his debts (always a problem with Caesar) were paid, and his next assignment awaited, and in 60 B.C. it arrived. Literally we beg a pardon for the usage of a time worn cliché, and that being that the man and the moment were about to meet.

GAUL

Julius Caesar began his famous and still extant commentaries on the Gallic Wars with a simple declarative statement memorized by untold generations of Latin students:

> "All Gaul is divided into three parts,
> one of which the Belgae inhabit,
> the Aquitani another,
> those who in their own language are all Celts,
> in ours Gauls, the third."

So began the text of a work composed intermittently over the years 59-51 B.C. wherein Caesar commanded legions of Roman soldiers, today themselves legendary, who conquered a entirety of modern-day France, Belgium, and Luxembourg. The <u>Commentaries</u> originally were dispatches sent by Caesar back to Rome, informing the Senate, officialdom and ordinary Romans of the works and adventures of the Roman legionaries under his command who had sent to Gaul in 59 B.C. Caesar, writing in the third person to describe himself, wisely and brilliantly maintained the tome of a dutiful soldier reporting back to his superiors on the fate of their soldiers. The Commentaries, written in ideal Latin prose would be read to crowds of Romans eager for news, and they enhanced and polished Caesar's reputation to the level, if not of a god, but a man with more talents than ordinary mortals. By the conclusion eight years later of the Gallic campaigns a strong case could be made that while still mortal, the talents, their depth, intensity, and variety, were far beyond those of ordinary men.

In 60 B.C. Caesar had been elected consul of Rome, and with the aid of his fellow oligarch (and monetary creditor), he had secured the governorship of Gaul, which at the time only a fraction of which was subject to Roman control. Caesar's nature did not provide for his recumbency in comfortable palaces or offices, and he determined to be an active governor of his new bailiwick. "Active" primarily noted, at least in this instance, military command, and so in Caesar political and military command both resided. Caesar through his just concluded Spanish venture had just enough military experience and luster to make such a command as he was to hold plausible.

At the beginning of Caesar's Gallic years, Gaul was in a state of flux, and this included both Roman and non-Roman Gaul. History's pages record that in this era many European people and tribes were beginning to migrate into Gaul and on a massive scale. These included other Gallic (Celtic people) Helvetü (from the region of modern Switzerland) and primarily Germanic tribes from the northeast. Rome and Caesar rightly saw this burgeoning of Gaul's population as a very real threat to continued Roman rule over Gaul. Early in his rule and command Caesar decided and committed to the conquest of the entirety of Gaul, which by European standards was a gargantuan area to subdue. The Gauls were not pushovers, and the tenacity and courage of Gallic warriors became legendary even to their enemies. Moreover, in terms of numbers the Gauls were decidedly superior to the Romans. Yet the Achilles' heel for the Gauls was their lack of unity and they had reluctance cooperating above the tribal level.

Caesar, with fewer men but excellent soldiers took advantage of this Gallic handicap. Throughout the mid-50's B.C. the Romans clashed with the Gauls in numerous battles which demonstrated not only Roman superiority but the capable military genius of Caesar, which he duly reported in continual dispatches from the front back to the home folks in Rome. Gaul was not falling to Roman weaponry, but it was beginning its long metamorphosis from a collection of Celts and Germans to a Romanized and Latin-based province and eventual nation. But Gaul did not go down easily to Caesar's legions. Eventually, yet too late, the Gauls found their leader, a man named Vercingetorix, the king of the Gallic tribe of Arveni, who united the Gauls in a last-ditch effort against Rome in 52 B.C. Vercingetorix won victories, but eventually his forces fell to Caesar's at Alesia in 51 B.C. The Gauls were defeated, Vercingetorix made a prisoner and the Romans under Caesar the unchallenged masters of all Gaul. The vengeful spirit of Caesar and his legions was on full display in the latter stage of the long Gallic War. Massive killings, rising to genocidal proportions, enslavement and grotesque punishments were meted out to the Gauls. As for Vercingetorix he was kept caged and finally brought to Rome as an ornament in Caesar's great triumph in 46 B.C., whereupon the Gallic leader was put to death for the amusements of the mob. Perhaps it was in respect to this time and these events that someone once made this statement:

"Julius Caesar would harm no man without purpose.
Yet, if he thought it necessary to advance his purposes
he could order the deaths of 50,000 men, women and children without concern."

Caesar's victory was staggering in scope, well publicized and gave to each loyal Roman a swelling sense of pride. He had done more than any Roman general ever, including Pompey, whose military prowess will be discussed in a later chapter. Now, the First Triumvirate formed in 60 B.C. was hanging by a thread and even then, in an attenuated form. Crassus, as recorded, had been killed by the Parthians in 53 B.C., and now it was 49 B.C.

In the wake of the Gallic campaign only two obstacles lay in the path of Julius Caesar. One was Pompey, the other surviving Triumvir, now aging but a figure of enormous prestige and power. By this stage in life, he was deeply ensconced into the Roman aristocracy and its power circles. Militarily, his record was not as current as Caesar's, but he could rightly pose as the man who made so much of Romer's eastern empire. He was still a dangerous foe, and much of the real power of Rome remained in his corner. The second of Caesar's obstacles was his own psychological proclivity. Would he cross over those barriers that Roman history traditionally had erected and proclaim himself king, dictator, or consul for life. His day of decision approached, and neither Rome nor the world would ever be the same.

THE RUBICON

For a decade Caesar had been absent from the city with which his name forever was manifest, perhaps to borrow a phrase from two millennia hence his "manifest destiny." Only the factual circumstances of that return remain to be settled. The only remaining Roman who could rival him in fame and more importantly in a large power base, was Pompey. Pompey, older than Caesar, had actually been the younger man's son-in-law for several years, having married Caesar's daughter, now deceased. Relations between these two titans had become strained, and it does not even require the hindsight of history to see that a clash between the two was looming.

It is perhaps misleading to aver that Pompey had become Caesar's enemy, for in such an assertion is a suggestion that he was Caesar's sole enemy. At this juncture of his career the great Julius Caesar had made so many enemies that their numbers defied quantification. In the Senate, still a powerful body, Caesar's foes were in the majority and were led by two of the most fabled Romans in history, Cato the Younger, and the greatest of all orators, Marcus Tullius Cicero. Their hearts remained with the old Republic, but their eyes could see that it was in danger of being supplanted by dictatorship, a role which apparently fitted Caesar life a glove. Too, they could sense that Caesar was shifting the gravity of Roman politics from being a strictly aristocratic ("patrician") domain to the non-noble plebian classes. With the oft proven enormity of his abilities the man might as well had the dread word "dictator" stamped upon him. Still, for the year 49 B.C. Caesar again secured the consulship, which when it expired in 48 B.C. would leave him a private citizen liable to prosecution from his inveterate enemies, a prosecution certain to come.

On January 7, 49 B.C., the Roman Senate ordered the nation's greatest soldier in all its history to disband his army and return to Rome, where he likely faced prosecution for crimes, real and imagined. At this time Caesar's famed army was camped at a small waterway in northern Italy which served as the boundary between Cisalpine Gaul (northern Italy) and the remainder of the country. The name of this river boundary was the Rubicon.

CHAPTER TEN – CROSSING THE RUBICON

To this day historians and geographers have never settled upon its exact location. The Rubicon River, hardly in the league of the Nile or Mississippi was a small stream among many such waterways in the north of Italy. Also, to this day not only to historians but to those few remaining who have some knowledge of antiquity the phrase "crossing the Rubicon" contains deep, even profound meaning. Whatever the obstacle and boundary lines of life a Rubicon is that line that when and if crossed, marks a stern point of demarcation a line when once crossed unlocks a new stage, even a new world which prevents the person(s) who cross and the wave of transients who follow no opportunity to return to the old.

Gaius Julius Caesar, now the greatest and most accomplished and celebrated figure alive, and perhaps in all Roman history stood on the banks of the Rubicon, and the fate of Rome rested upon his decision. Disband the army, submit to the Senate, face a trial for insubordination and treason with his own death as its terminus, or the alternative, ignore a legally given dictate, gather his large, superbly trained, and experienced army, and cross the Rubicon as his prelude to marching upon Rome? From the retrospective of our perch two millennia hence such a question seems almost self-mocking, for the answer could only be that which promised the most gain to Caesar. He was a man, now fifty-one years of age, a patient man who had endured years of hard service and hardship, political infighting always with the implied risk of death in case of defeat and always with a self-knowledge and self-assurance that he was better, smarter, and stronger than other men. To add to the laurels of his political skills was an ability to disguise and secret personal pride and ambition behind a screen of service to the Roman state. Caesar's life had been a half century's drive for power, and here not just power alone but the sweet promise of absolute power was the succulent fruit that hung low on the Roman tree. Besides, so successful had he been that at this crossroads in Caesar's life laws and Senatorial edicts were for lesser men to obey, certainly not Caesar.

The great Julius Caesar with his magnificent army crossed the Rubicon, and once more the Roman state and people were to engage in self-inflicted slaughter. Crossing the Rubicon was the opening volley in a Roman Civil War, just as assuredly as was the firing upon Fort Sumter two thousand years later was the opening bell for the civil war of an even greater state. Now all that stood between Julius Caesar and absolute power, sole authority in the Roman state, was the "non-Caesar" portion of the Roman army, the command of which the Senate had entrusted to the other remaining triumvir, Pompey. At age fifty-seven Pompey was past his prime, but his skills remained formidable and when hitched to the core of the Roman army, Caesar's foe was worthy. Besides, for whatever its value Pompey retained the support of the bulk of the Roman establishment. Further, for all his fame, skill, glory and glamour, Caesar was still an interloper attempting to overthrow an existing order, or at least bend that order to his desires, never an easy task. Or so it would appear.

Within three months after being entrusted with the army's command by the Senate, Caesar had so outmaneuvered Pompey that the former Young Butcher fled to the temporary safety of Greece. All Italy now lay subservient to Caesar, but most of the population did not see it in this fashion. The Italian populace confronted the merciful

Caesar, who went easy on his former enemies, winning many to his side, and the popular feeling undeniably was growing, even burgeoning, in Caesar's favor. Caesar now had the political power and military momentum to have himself appointed dictator. It was not all laurels and triumphs, though, for Pompey's forces still retained a powerful sting. Caesar followed Pompey to Greece in 48 B.C., but he was rebuffed in battle. Instead of risking a climatic battle with Pompey, though, Caesar withdrew his forces to Spain. Regaining his battlefield mastery Caesar defeated the Pompeian forces which were based in Spain. Finally, Caesar turned from Iberia and traveled to Greece and faced his one-time fellow triumvir and confidante in a major decisive, eve landmark battle. At a place called Pharsalus derisively defeated Pompey. Immediately Caesar's victory paid political dividends, for he was again named dictator for another year.

For the time, now into the winter of 48 B.C. Caesar was otherwise occupied with other civil and military manners that demanded his attention, and Pompey was allowed to escape, presumably to Egypt. With his forces Caesar traveled to Egypt to establish and fortify his new mistress, Cleopatra VII, on the throne of Egypt and hopefully crush Pompey once and for all. Sometime following his arrival in Egypt, though, Caesar discovered that his combat with Pompey was in the past, as he was presented the severed head of his one-time friend son-in-law, fellow triumvir, and conspirator. Other smaller actions followed, but as much as any man or woman who ever lived Caesar had effectively gathered all real temporal power unto himself. But for how long would it be his?

By whatever name he called himself or bid others to call him the power of Julius Caesar was unlike anything seen before in the centuries long history of Rome. Be he king, emperor, consul, first citizen or whatever else his adoring and groveling coterie of followers could invent all the reins of power were in his hands. He had the army, almost all the Senate and more importantly he had widespread popular support that continued to grow. For the moment Caesar himself was content with the simple appellation of "Dictator for Life." The scope of this work will not admit a detailed discussion of Caesar's work over the following two years. In general, he tried to expand the availability of the justice system to all, consolidate all the Italian peninsular provinces into a single Roman or Italian entity, provide more generous benefits to army veterans and to broaden both the base of land ownership and prosperity.

Still, many had become sick of Julius Caesar. By obvious purpose the words "Rome" and "Caesar" were becoming synonyms, and the great, storied Roman Republic was fading into the darkening shadows of an historical relic. More personally, though, no man achieves such fame and power, especially over such a long period, without acquiring a host of enemies. Caesar's enemies were legion, and for his own good they were concentrated in the worst of all places, the Roman Senate, still a body of the most powerful of Romans outside Caesar's personal chain of command. It has been variously estimated that from sixty to ninety Senators were part of the conspiracy, that intrigue which led to the most notorious of all political murders. The prime movers, though, were winnowed down to two long time associates to themselves and generals subordinate to Caesar himself, Cassius and Brutus.

In 44 B.C. on March 15 (the famed Ides of March) the Senate would be in session, and it would be meeting at the Theater of Pompey, still an honored (but defeated and dead Caesarian opponent) figure in Rome. Today was special as Julius Caesar himself would be present and a participant in the Senate's agenda. When he arrived, he was momentarily distracted by a man named Trebonius, who on bended knee pleaded the remission of a sentence of exile upon his brother. As his unsuccessful pleading proceeded Casca, another senator and in the inner circle of the conspiracy quickly and deftly deflected the blow whereupon the frightened Casca called for help. A large, but unspecified in numbers band of dignified Senators rushed upon Caesar, whereupon hey resorted to street thuggery and hacked, cut, and sliced him to death. As immortalized by Shakespeare the dying Caesar saw that one of the blows had been delivered by Brutus, a hitherto loyal subordinate, and a man for whom Caesar had some affection. He gasped his last breath which contained his own benediction of "Et tu Brute," or "You, too, Brutus." The body of Julius Caesar then fell lifeless to the floor next to a statue of Pompey. To each individual reader is left the depths and extent of the justice, injustice, or irony such a death at the foot of Pompey conjures in his mind. Gaius Julius Caesar, to this day two millennia later, the most famous of all Romans, was dead. After sixteen long, gruesome bloody years the First Triumvirate of Crassus, Pompey and Caesar had found its end. Crassus and Pompey met violent battle connected ends and were recipients of the ignominy of being beheaded. The chopped, minced, and diced body of Caesar had received a total of twenty-three stab wounds. It is unlikely, nay impossible, that any of this group of elegant, Latin speaking, powerful Senators who milled about the body of Julius Caesar would have grasped the meaning of the words of a Galilean carpenter uttered some seventy years hence:

"All they that take the sword shall perish with the sword."

The three great colossi of mid-first century B.C. were gone, but the power that they, especially Caesar wielded remained. It would not lie untouched for long, and Rome, the magnificent western power, was about to descend into yet another generation of civil war.

The conspirators, primarily Brutus and Cassius, both experienced generals, had to be considered. Neither, though, seemed to have that insatiable lust for personal power that so distinguished their predecessors, not just the First Triumvirate, but men such as Marius and Sulla. Brutus, one of history's true tragic figures, was really republican to the core, and he idealized the old Roman Republic, an entity which was growing increasingly irrelevant and finally defunct. The popularity which Caesar retained even in death turned into bitter enemies towards the conspirators, so Brutus and Cassis fled to the east, specifically to Greece. There, they raised a huge army, many from the thousands of veterans only temporarily unemployed from the conclusion of the earlier civil war. Not only the acquisition of power was in play, though, because events in Rome clarified that the lives of Brutus and Cassius were at risk.

Quickly the Second Triumvirate had arisen on the heels of Caesar's death and funeral. The three whose identities became clear were Marcus Antonius (82-30 BC), known to history as Mark Antony, Marcus Aemilius Lepidus, a former consul, and Gaius Octavius (63 BC – AD 12), whose apparent sole qualification for office was that he was Julius Caesar's grandnephew. Further, he was only nineteen years of age with no real experience I the rough and tumble, play for keeps, world of Roman politics at the highest level. Yet... he was the legal heir of Julius Caesar and could rightly bear that magical name of Caesar. Like all political alliances it was makeshift and bore an air of uneasiness. Antony easily was the best known, one of Caesar's most trusted commanders in Gaul, a somewhat glamorous figure who nevertheless to the present day has historically carried a certain thuggish image. If the Romans wagered on such matters (and most assuredly they did) he would have been the early betting favorite to succeed to total power.

If ever an ancient city was fated for fame, it was Philippi, capital of ancient Macedonia. Named for King Philip, the fabled but certainly real leader of the ancient Macedonians, a half-Greek, half-barbarian people north of mainland Greece it became the cockpit of Philip's kingdom and later similarly for his still more famous son, Alexander the Great. Later in the first century when the sun's radiance shined more on Rome it became famous as the locale for one of the strongest bodies of early Christians and a scene of dramatic notoriety for the church's greatest evangelist. In between lay the battle of Philippi. After Brutus and Cassius fled Rome for the temporary haven of Greece and Macedonia, Antony and Octavian followed with their armies, and found Brutus and Cassius with smaller forces but yet set in a strong, advantageous position. At first Antony drove back the forces of Cassius, who committed suicide, while Brutus's army then routed the troops of Octavian. After the irresolution of this initial contest, Brutus renewed the battle, was totally defeated, and committed suicide. Literary and historical immortality awaited Brutus, for centuries later the great Shakespeare concludes his work "Julius Caesar" with the victorious Antony standing over the body of Brutus and remarking that "This was the noblest Roman of all."

While the memory of the tragic Brutus awaited immortality, a different fate was that day sealed for the Roman Republic. For decades it had writhed in a slow ballet of death, but its fate was finalized at Philippi. For years oratorical lip service would be paid to the memo0ry of the Republic, but as a living entity it had expired. Now and for the next five hundred years real power would fall into the hands of emperors, would-be emperors and/or their armies. The old Roman Republic was gone, and for the moment what remained was the Second Triumvirate of three men, Antony, Octavian, and Lepidus. The three quickly secured a Senatorial appointment to formally rule as the Second Triumvirate for a period of five years, an eternity in Roman politics.

The triumvirs set immediately to work with the historically infamous lists of proscriptions, a roster of names of those which any or all of the triumvirs had identified as enemies worthy of death. The most famous of the victims of proscription was the great orator and Senator Cicero. Quickly it became apparent that the real power in the Triumvirate was confined to Antony and Octavian Lepidus – was certainly not the insignificant cipher often depicted in history or in historical fiction, for he was a trusted and competent general under

Caesar himself. His only power base was his own army command, but by 36 BC they had deserted him for Octavian. Lepidus then whether by force or choice was compelled to retire from the scene, and he faded from history.

Mark Antony was not a man to fade away from anything, but he soon discovered to his chagrin that young Octavian was not necessarily a callow youth, but rather a rising star who seemed to have an inborn deft political touch, all the while possessing the majestic and magical name of Caesar. The political situation was so dynamic that it could retain no sense of certainty and purpose. Octavian, though as hungry for power as Antony or any other, gained the support of the Senate and within a couple of years of Philippi the situation, both personally and politically had been greatly altered. The Roman world was divided, with Octavian receiving the West and Antony the East. Also, in 40 B.C. the two triumvirs became relatives when Antony married Octavian's sister Octavia (a not uncommon practice with the Roman aristocracy and ruling class). Unsurprisingly, Antony, a life-long adulterer practically to the point of being a satyr, found his eye beginning to wander. Its brightness was shining when it alit upon Caesar's former mistress, Queen Cleopatra, Egypt and hence began perhaps history's most famous and ill-fated love affair.

As befitted their personalities the next few years were witness to more obviously overt activity from Antony than from Octavian. Antony's liaison with Cleopatra had begun in 41 B.C. but had been temporarily interrupted by his marriage to Octavia. It soon resumed, and to the apparent political benefit of each. Cleopatra's rule in Egypt was highly unstable, and she welcomed the strength and sense of legitimacy which Rome would provide. By bolstering Cleopatra and Egypt Antony gained the enormous wealth, primarily agricultural, which he and his forces would enjoy. Besides in spite of all the historical and dramatic flummery that he has attached to this affair it appears that Antony actually did love Cleopatra. He was still a Roman ruler and a general by trade, and his services were on continuous call. His record was mixed. An enemy in the East, the nation of Pontus, threatened the Roman realm in 37 B.C., but Antony was unsuccessful in subduing this foe. In 36 B.C., though, he was successful in subduing Armenia, whereupon as a conqueror, he returned not to Rome but to Egypt's capital, Alexandria, in triumph.

Antony had success in securing allies in the East, most notably a man named Herod, who was the son of Antipater, the king of a land bordering Judea known as Idumean. When Antipater died in 37 B.C., this talented ruler, soon to become known for his success as a builder (among other things) was named as King of Judea, pledging his loyalty, friendship, and fealty to Antony.

After defeating the Armenians Antony's return to Egypt marked the true dawn of the period, fact, and mythology of "Antony and Cleopatra." He, a man of Rome, the city which had made not without truth, the reputation of plain living and an eschewal of the vices of soft living, divided into a period of Oriental splendor, or perhaps grotesque debauchery as may be interpreted. Roman officials, governors, consuls and the like doubtless lived comfortable lives in comfortable homes, but under the Republic conspicuousness with success was not considered a virtue. Not only this but the hostility of many Romans of all classes was intensified by their knowledge that Antony was doing it all with a foreign mistress. Although the Roman culture was changing traditional Romans had long placed high value on what might be called republican simplicity. Antony's lifestyle was becoming a flagrant, cynical rejection of Roman traditions and mores, and worst of all he was doing so in a strange foreign land while coupled adulterously with a foreign woman. (For the record, Cleopatra, while Queen of Egypt, was Greek by ethnicity). Young Mark Antony, while once the glamorous, ruggedly handsome commander at the right hand of Julius Caesar himself was now a fast-aging dissipating rogue who had not even seen Rome for years. His popularity and the streaking star that had been his promise and career seemingly had reached its apogee. Still, his command included one-half the Roman realm.

At the beginning of 33 B.C. the agreement of Rome's division between Antony and Octavian came to an end. Further within the ensuing year Antony divorced Octavia, and of course, Antony and Octavian ceased being brothers-in-law. The two famed Romans, though, remained the world's dual centers of power, but it is more than the luxury of the removal of two millennia of time to aver that any observer could see that the days of this dual "monarchy" were numbered.

As far as we know Mark Antony first met young Octavian after the assassination of the latter's great uncle Julius Caesar in 44 B.C. Antony, a hardened experienced battle commander was likely underwhelmed by the young Octavian, jut nineteen, not particularly impressive physically and lacking in political and military experience. Surely must Antony have conjectured that Octavian would be ripe for simply sweeping aside on Antony's climb to absolute power. It would not happen, and whatever were Antony's first impressions of young Octavian events and years should have given him reckoning that Octavian was certainly not now (and perhaps never had been) any innocent youth playing in a political league beyond his reach. Here in 32 B.C., Octavian was still youthful, but at age thirty-one he had been steeled a bit himself. His youthfulness had always been in tandem with a naturally serious demeanor and approach to persons and affairs which served him well. Since appearing on the scene, he had demonstrated no special charisma but rather abilities, both political and personal, which were increasingly noted, and which served him well. Of all his assets maybe two should be briefly mentioned for special acclaim. If not, a natural he soon enveloped a natural inclination towards politics and the political class, and it is likely that he was known more for his ability than his youth. He gladly, and with a least some sincerity, assumed the mantel of the defender of traditional, conservative Roman ways, of which he was proud. The contrast between Octavian (though his own life was sullied with a fair share of taint) and Antony, who was continually debauching himself with a foreign queen could not have been greater.

Octavian's possession of the heirship of the man already proclaimed as the greatest in Roman history and the very name Caesar must never be undervalued. The name and heirship always bestowed upon Octavian a certain legitimacy which was lacking in Mark Antony.

By 31 B.C. the tide of Roman affairs was definitely moving in Octavian's direction, but as yet nothing was a fait accompli. Mark Antony still ruled half the Roman world and could count upon enormous resources for whatever action, whether by choice or dictated by circumstances, lay ahead. Official and popular feeling had so pivoted against Antony that by 31 B.C. Octavian believed it was time to declare a national Roman war against Antony and Cleopatra. Once again it appeared that the famed contestants who lusted for power would meet on a date certain for a historical resolution of the contest. As Caesar met Pompey at Pharsalus and Brutus and Cassius faced Antony and Octavian at Philippi so the latter two would meet at Actium. Yet, this time the setting, the situation and even the outcome would not go as some already scripted play.

Mark Antony, still possessed of conspicuous military skills had moved his military and naval forces to Epirus, on the west coast of Greece. There, he stymied the forces of Octavian and his right-hand man, Marcus Agrippa. For reasons that retain an historical unclarity in August 31 B.C., Antony decided to force the issue, but surprisingly by way of a naval contest at Actium off the Greek coast. The engagement commenced early in the morning, and at first matters seemed to be swaying in favor of Antony, when all collapsed. The fleet of sixty Egyptian ships, which had sailed at Cleopatra's command turned and abandoned the contest. Then, the great Mark Antony commander of the fleet, ruler of one-half the Roman world and the protégé of Julius Caesar himself deserted his command, giving to Octavian one of history's greatest and most important victories. Antony escaped back to Alexandria, but defeated and dispirited, he chose the route of suicide. Octavian arrived an when it became apparent that she would be hauled back to Rome as a defeated barbarian queen and made an object of mockery and derision in a Roman triumph she, too, took her own life.

Octavian returned to Rome, literally with the world, or at least Rome's section of it, at his feet. From a neophyte nineteen-year-old he had developed and could legitimately lay claim to be the world's most powerful man, as powerful as his storied uncle Julius Caesar and with a base of rule and power more secure. He soon laid down his dictatorial authority and took instead the traditional title of consul of Rome. Wise, temperate, and circumspect still he had no aim of abandoning power and from 27 B.C. to A.D. 14 he would rule as imperator, the first true emperor of Rome. He would do so under the new name now bestowed upon, Augustus Caesar, and under this name and rule he would bring to Rome its greatest glories ever. Throughout his forty year reign many babies would be born into a world ruled by Augustus, and he would reign over an empire that he has inherited, partially made, and successfully consolidated. Our story will rejoin the lifetime and reign of Augustus Caesar in two chapters hence, but for now let us pause in our own Augustin narrative and credit it to him the bringing of a special gift which all those babies, and one obscure Galilean infant in particular would enjoy from birth – peace.

CHAPTER ELEVEN – PEACE IN ROME: WAR IN JUDEA

So, at last, the Roman world had peace. After a century's worth of ferociously ambitions and talented men (and a woman or two) Rome began a peace so long, definite and pronounced that in retrospect the next one to two hundred years bears the title of the Pax Romana, or the "Roman Peace." Many questions spring from this chapter's first two sentences, but briefly we will give attention to two, and to fairly accomplish such a task we must venture on the road of a brief retrospective journey from 27 B.C., where Chapter Ten concluded. The first question is simple and easy to answer. What was the Roman world utilizing the year 70 B.C., as a touchstone the reasons for which will become apparent the Roman world then consisted of Italy, Greece, Macedonia, Egypt, much of the northern Africa, a substantial portion of Spain and a small section of Gaul (modern France). The career of Julius Caesar has been reviewed in some detail, and by the conclusion of his life inn 44 B.C., what would become the western Roman Empire had been gained and consolidated y Caesar. It included the Iberian Peninsula (modern Spain and Portugal), all of the large expanse of Gaul, Belgium, Luxembourg, the southern portion of the island of Britain and Germany up to the west bank of the Rhine River. Such an empire, with Rome as its capital, would seem to be grossly imbalanced to the west, as in the east in 70 B.C. Rome had only Greece and Macedonia, and a few other possessions. Such a situation did not arise, though, because before the west of Europe felt the martial tread of Caesar's legions the east had seen and succumbed to the martial skills of one of the other famous Triumvirs, Pompey. The roots of this impending eastern conquests are not anchored to any great storied land or nation led by an historically renown general. The roots of conquest originally were of necessity anchored in salt water, the eastern Mediterranean Sea to be precise. Rome was a city not entirely self-sufficient, and it relied on steady commerce from other regions, east, west, north, and south, to sustain its living standard and burgeoning growth. That commerce had begun to suffer substantially and with an increasing destruction by an ever-present peril of sea travel, piracy. With the word "piracy" images of Captain Hook, Blackbeard, Captain Kidd, and Lon John Silver leap to the screen of the modern mind. This was different. The pirates of the ancient Mediterranean formed an organization for criminal enterprise (think modern Mafia), and they were choking Roman commerce. The Romans, who rarely let any problem fester for long, quickly dispatched their leading military luminary, Pompey, to the east in 67 B.C. Such was not done without major opposition, for although Pompey did not have absolute power, he was referred to as Primus Inter Pares ("First among equals"), and his acquisition of more power and acclaim was rightly seen as a possible gateway to dictatorship. Nonetheless, Pompey's talent, reputation and power were too great to be denied, and he was dispatched to the east with both naval and military forces under his command. Three months later in 67 B.C. his already bright reputation had been burnished to dazzling proportions, as the pirates had been defeated, some even joining the Romans as new allies.

Rome's power in the east now seemed to be beyond challenge, although such situations rarely deter both the foolhardy or the daring. Our narrative has previously mentioned Mithridates of Pontus, one of antiquities greatest rulers and military leaders. Pontus formed basically the center section of the Anatolian Empire (modern Turkey) and had been at odds with Rome for some time. Once and for all, though, Pompey defeated his and added his country to his and Rome's trophy room.

Now, on the southeastern coast of the Mediterranean Rome's next two prizes were ripe, the ancient and storied, but now weak in the face of Rome's might, lands of Syria and Phoenicia. Pompey and his army were poised immediately north of the tiny contemptible land of Judea, home to a naturally intelligent but truculent population, a religion incomprehensible to most Gentiles but one which the Jews themselves seemed to alternately ignore or fight over. In 63 B.C. Judea was far from calm, and once again its people were at war with one another. In answer to the second question of why did the Romans take Judea the proper response is likely a combination of many factors, but perhaps most of all the realization that it would be dangerous for Rome to ignore and leave for others a province at was with itself and therein be a threat to peace.

Almost all nations, empires, states, federations, etc. have always been subject to factionalism, the most severe version of which explodes in civil war. It is not anti-Semitism to record that among people and ethnicities the Jews were in the front rank of this practice. In 63 B.C. the Jews were engaged in such a struggle. From their heroic ascendancy in the 160's B.C. the Maccabees had been in the ascendancy, politically and culturally, in Judea. Now, more commonly called the Hasmoneans they had long had their grasp upon the office of the high priest. By this point in their centuries long reign the Hasmoneans themselves were subject to bitter in-fighting. By the time the arrival of Pompey and his legions in 63 B.C. the Jews had been locked in a civil war between two Hasmonean factions which centered around two brothers, Aristobulus II and Hyrcanus II. Both had been high priests but Aristobulus for both the longest tenure and the present. The contest was bloody (the irony of killing for religious position does not here go unmentioned), and the contest was even between the two factions. Although it is very much an over-simplification it must be recognized that two Jewish religious sects, each of which will become more prominent and important with each page of this narrative were among the prime movers of this war. Generally, the Sadducees favored Aristobulus and the Pharisees, Hyrcanus, whose orientation was generally Sadducean.

The civil war between the two factions, both self-defined by their greater devotion to God continued, but the Romans had arrived. It is somewhat to paint with a glossy brush gory and sordid battle and bloodshed, but in the greater interests of the narrative's pace we must. The Sadducean forces with Aristobulus as their champion were besieged within the walls of the city of Jerusalem by a force composed of their fellow Jews, mainly Pharisees, and the Roman legions under Pompey, at this time the greatest general of the age. Ancient historians record that some 12,000 Jews died in the siege of Jerusalem, an impressive (more properly, a depressive number) when we consider that ancient Jerusalem was a small situs, with a land area of no more than four to six square miles. As terrible and repellent as such bloodshed and slaughter must have been, though, it was a mere prelude and down payments on the total destruction which the city would receive from the Romans over a century later.

But for now, to the victor belong the spoils. General and Consul Pompey had received another bright, glittering star in his crown of impressive conquests on behalf of the people and Senate of Rome. After suffering so fiercely and for so long it is unlikely that the city of Jerusalem made much of an impression upon its conquerors from the West. One building, though, still stood forth, the pride of the Jews and the one locale which veritably demanded the attentions of any visitor, much less a conquering general. That was the Temple itself, the very heart of Judaism an its worship of an exceedingly strange monotheistic Deity. Pompey himself had personally come to Jerusalem because one of the Jewish contestants for power, Aristobulus had promised to pay Pompey for Roman help but had reneged on the promise. Pompey had then named his opponent Hyrcanus II as the new high priest. Apparently, it bothered neither Hyrcanus nor his followers neither a jot nor a title that religious matters had been so compromised that a pagan Gentile was naming the occupant of the office originally held by Moses's brother Aaron and ordained by God Himself.

As for Pompey himself the day came when naturally he wanted to view the prizes that he had won. What had the blood of his own soldiers, and 12,000 Jews purchased him to wear as an additional feather in his hat? No place would be more revelatory to Pompey than the Temple itself but also the most sacred room in the Temple, the Holy of Holies, so named by God Himself in Mosaic times. To the Jews such a visit presented to them an insoluble problem for the Holy of Holies was forbidden except for one day a year, the Day of Atonement, and then to one man only, the High Priest, who would make offering for the sins of the people. Pompey was no high priest, not even a Jew, and these certain eccentricities and trivialities of Jewish Law mattered not a whit to him. He would come and view for himself the fruits of his victory.

The day of the imperial visit came, and remarkably for ancient history we have been provided accounts by three famous historians, the Romans Plutarch and Cassius Dio and the great Jewish chronicler, Josephus. For clarity and simplicity our account of Pompey's visit to the Holy of Holies is taken at length from the account of Josephus:

> "For Pompey went into (the inaccessible parts of the Temple)
> and not a few of those who were with him also
> and saw all that which it was unlawful for other men to see,
> but only for the High Priests.
>
> There were in the temple the golden table,
> the holy candlestick,

> and the pouring vessels;
> and a great quantity of spices:
> and besides these there were among the treasures,
> two thousand talents of sacred money.
>
> Yet did Pompey say nothing of all this;
> an account of his regard to religion;
> and in this point also he acted in a manner that was worthy of his virtue.
> The next day he gave order to those that had the charge of the temple
> to cleanse it, and to bring what offerings the law required to God,
> and restored the High Priesthood to Hyrcanus."

Pompey and the military and civil entourage which trailed him should not have ever set foot in the Holy of Holies. Still, it is difficult not to acknowledge a rough type of grudging acknowledgment of good intentions to the Jews's new Roman master. At this time in its history Rome had imbibed from vast wars and conquests a type of wise experience that led them to a belief that it was Rome's best interest to leave untouched a people's religion. For at least a hundred years more, Rome essentially followed these precepts as it sought a minimum of trouble from its provinces. Its two main concerns were keeping the Roman peace and the collection of as much revenue as possible, each of which they did with noted efficiency. Pompey, the maker of much of the eastern Roman Empire was by this stage of his career a prime exemplar of Roman policy.

Only Pompey could have answered the queries as to what realms his thoughts visited when he witnessed the most sacred and venerated "shrine" of the Jews. But what may God have seen and thought when he viewed Pompey? He, of course, saw a pagan Gentile who knew not the one true God, yet the world had always been abundant with the heathen who dwelled in darkness. God saw power in Pompey, a real, authentic power which Rome had spent centuries gathering and which was still on the upward trajectory to its pinnacle. He saw the results of Roman planning, labor, diligence, and discipline which led its armies from another continent now becoming masters of the small outpost of His Chosen, the Jews. Perhaps He saw in Pompey's tour of the Holy of Holies what in retrospect seems apparent to the modern eye. God saw that for better or for worse the Roman world and the Jewish world, politically, culturally, and even religiously had now found its nexus, its point of linkage which would be the backdrop for the most important scenes of all Creation's endless history. Rome and the remainder of the world would be bathed in the Light which was to come some sixty years later. The scenic stage for the world of the New Testament was now set.

Of course, this which is open to our eyes in the Christian Age was unknown by all, Roman or Jew, Pompey, priest, or pauper at this moment. Yet God knew and knew that His plans were working themselves forward to a scene in which He, the Romans and the Jewish religious establishment would be in the forefront of the dramatic personae. Pompey had done more than gain yet another province, Judea, small as it was, for Rome. He had found and begun the linkage of not just the Roman, but the entire Gentile world to the Plan of Redemption which would eventually be forthcoming in the Jerusalem which his legionaries had just subdued. Pompey, who undoubtedly had never even heard His name, had taken a giant stride forward in preparing the world for its Savior.

For now, though, the mundane affairs of organizing yet another state which had befallen the great leviathan of the West, Rome. The Romans, of course, left in question that they were now in charge, and to the chagrin and even agony of most of the Jewish people the weight of foreign government began to fall upon them. Roman rule, north, south, east, or west always was marked by a certain consistency. The tax system was reorganized, and the wealth, productivity and riches of the Jewish population began to enter the pipelines of servitude which all led to Rome. Yet, the Jewish nation, albeit unwillingly for the most part, received nor little recompense from the Romans. Their western masters brought stability, law and order, and no foreign power could or would dare challenge Rome's rule. It is a prized commodity, this "stability" which people rarely discuss and just as commonly overlook when it is missing but which becomes a most lamented virtue when it is gone. The Romans, at times harsh, brought this cherished good. The Jews, of course, saw much of their productive labors expropriated and refashioned to the service of Rome, yet evidence exists that Judea was enjoying prosperity under its Roman masters. Likely this was due to the consistent rule the Romans provided and also the natural intelligence and proclivity to hard work which were (and are) seemingly endemic to the Jewish people. Stability and prosperity are desirable, and a prolonged period of both helps to reconcile persons and even entire populations to their ruling governments. We hope to note the effects it had upon the Jews.

The immediacy of certain needs demanded Pompey's attention in the aftermath of his great victory. As the historian Josephus noted his orders to cleanse the temple (in a literal sense) were followed, and to a large, though not a perfect degree, it was the beginning of a period of respect, although often permeated with disdain, that marked the Roman attitude towards Judaism. So long as the Jews, a different sort with which the Romans had ever dealt, gave loyalty and tribute to Rome, in turn the Romans followed a hands-off policy towards their religion, a religion not only strange to the Romans but often incomprehensible.

It must not be forgotten that the foreigners, Pompey and his Romans, were working in the aftermath of a civil war, always a ghastly affair and a giant obstacle to restoring order and stability. As expected, Pompey restored Hyrcanus II to the office of the High Priest, a post for which he had literally fought for years. At this juncture it is imperative to note the decline of the Jewish nation from the ideals and laws which God, through Moses, had laid before them some fourteen hundred years previously. The office of High Priest was instituted by God Himself, announced on Mt. Sinai, and given to Aaron, the older brother of Moses, and was to pass through his descendants in the Tribe of Levi. Now, it has become a political plum, fought over, killed over, and eventually a political prize appointed by a heathen Gentile general. So, it would remain, even and especially through New Testament times. From this moment on not only Hyrcanus but all Jewish High Priests served at the pleasure of the Romans. This is a reality central not only to the New Testament story but to all history which follows.

So, Hyrcanus II had emerged the victor over his brother Aristobulus II and would serve as High Priest with all the pomp, splendor, power, and glory which the secular government of Rome concurred. He would not serve, though, as King of Judea, a title which he also held before the arrival of the Romans but an appellation which the Romans were reluctant to confer upon anybody. Hyrcanus, though, who held the High Priesthood for an exceptionally long period of time could find solace in finally achieving an additional title in 47 B.C. By that time Julius Caesar controlled all power, and he name Hyrcanus "ethnarch," a name and an office possessing a certain sheen of blurred fuzziness. It meant the ruler of an ethnic group, the Jews, but essentially carried no authority and power, and in time was abolished. Hyrcanus, though, had another meaningless title to add to his historical resume.

Maybe much of Hyrcanus II was essentially meaningless. Originally Pompey favored Hyrcanus over Aristobulus in the Jewish Civil War primarily because he was older, friendlier to the Romans and would be more pliable in office. Pompey, though, soon left the Jewish religions and cultural scene and returned to the high stakes' world of Roman power politics. Hyrcanus, though, was not alone for he had acquired an advisor, counselor, mentor, and the very embodiment of the quintessential "man behind the throne," a man eventually known as Antipater I the Idumaean (113 B.C. – 43 B.C.). Antipater was from Edom, the region southeast of Judah and founded by the Old Testament patriarch Esau. As he emerged into politics, he masterfully bestrod two worlds, the Roman and the Jewish, well connected in both. He held high positions not only under Hyrcanus but other Hasmonean priests. Among other traits Antipater proved to be a political chameleon of the highest (or perhaps "lowest"), and his associates and patrons reads almost as a Who's Who of ancient Roman luminaries. Whether it is counted as good or evil fortune much of Antipater's prime political years was spent in a time of fluidity and rapid changes in not only the world of Jewish politics but of the highest strata of Roman government, the two now being interwoven for the foreseeable future.

The later years of the Hasmonean dynasty, coupled with, perhaps even overwhelmed by the coming of the Romans, was a time of great confusion in Jewish politics, and likely in the main this was of great benefit to a man such as Antipater. As we have noted he was the real local ruling power in Judea, even while Hyrcanus II held the title of king. The shelves are filled with history books which describe in great detail the radical changes which were occurring in the highest ether of Roman politics, which our essay has described with brevity. Antipater's great political "break" came when Julius Caesar defeated Pompey, Antipater's former patron, in the Roman Civil War. Wisely, Antipater then came to Caesar's aid at Alexandria, Egypt, and for this succulent political plum of chief ministries to Judea fell into his hands. The title alone was a prize worth having, but the real lasting reward was that Antipater was now charged with and given the right to collect taxes from his realm. For such a monumental task Antipater needed the assistance of trusted subordinates, and for this he had two sons, Pharsalus, who was appointed governor of Jerusalem and the other the new governor of Galilee, Herod. This was the Herod whose name would live in the infancy of history as Herod the Great.

The days of Antipater were running short, though, and he himself effectively became a victim of the bloody whirlpool of Roman power politics. Demonstrating the dexterity which is an integral part of the corpus of the finest political animal, upon Caesar's assassination Antipater became a friend and ally of one of the two chief assassins, Cassius. Cassius, though, was soon cornered by Mark Antony and Octavian and slew himself. Somehow, though, Antipater regained the confidence and favor of mark Antony. At the end, though, the increasingly enthusiastic Roman political bent of Antipater did him no personal good, and in 43 B.C., he died of poison, likely at the hands of a murderer.

The time of Antipater's death saw the Roman political world immersed in powerful, titanic struggles, which have been previously and hopefully with adequacy, described. Soon, the great breadth of the world which Rome ruled and influenced was divided into two realms, the west under Octavian and the east at the command of Mark Antony, who was assisted by his mistress, the famed Queen of Egypt, Cleopatra. Although we may be accused of relying upon the infallibility of hindsight likely even at the time most observers knew that such an arrangement had a limited lifespan and that either Antony or Octavian would gain full control. The average person was but a shuttlecock, whipped by the winds of fate, time and events, but a certain few were required to cast their lot with one or other of the two leaders. Such a man was Herod, the tetrarch of Galilee.

At the outset Herod rolled his dice on Antony's side of the table, and even, without solicitation, rendered him military assistance in Antony's campaign against the Parthians. With the backing of Mark Antony Herod began to sense that any real constraints upon his power were beginning to fall aside, and he acted accordingly. Early in Herod's reign Antigonus, the last of the Hasmonean line, perished at the executioner's dock, thus ending the Hasmonean reign begun by the family of the Maccabees some one hundred twenty-five years earlier. Although Herod had grasped great power it was hardly unfettered, for especially in the first years of his reign his enemies were so numerous as to be difficult to list. First, he still had the recent past wit which to contend. Old Antigonus still had followers, especially among the aristocracy, but Herod dispatched some forty-five of them by execution.

The Hasmonean family itself, so powerful for over a century, especially his own mother-in-law Alexandra and her son, another Aristobulus who Herod appointed as high priest. Herod, whose propensity towards the savagery of ruthless violence was already well developed later had Aristobulus drowned and was even persuasive in getting Mark Antony to imprison Alexandra, who was humiliatingly placed in chains. Although Herod maintained a canine degree of loyalty to Antony, the latter's famous mistress, Cleopatra, still loathed this upstart.

Certainly not to be omitted is the animosity which most of the Jewish people felt for Herod. He was not a Jew, and ethnically not really even a half-Jew but a Idumeanean. Those Jews who did side with Herod would be well rewarded, but it was a love-hate relationship which would be perpetuated for decades.

On the grander stage of world politics Herod had little influence but rather the strength of his throne and power was highly sensitive to grand events. Upon the defeat of Antony at Actium in 31 B.C., Herod was bereft of his sponsor and protector. With the speed of a gazelle and the reptilian treachery of a snake Herod immediately sought to boost his own standing with Octavian, soon to be Augustus, the sole ruler of Rome. Herod executed all the surviving Hasmoneans upon whom he could lay his hands, thereby eliminating a temptation of the Romans to return to the old ruling regime. He met the future emperor at Rhodes and persuasively convinced him of his loyalty to Octavian.

By now Herod, known to us all as Herod the Great had become King of all Judea. Yet Herod still had in his future a very important, lengthy, and lurid role to play in the story of Judea, and of course, its poor northern cousin, Galilee. As with Rome upon the ascension of Augustus to the emperor's throne this small province of Judea would enjoy a long period devoid of wars. It cannot comfortably be called peace, though, because the hearts and spirits of so many Jews were at war with one another and with God. A generation later Herod the Great would reappear at the commencement of the New Testament chronicle, but it was into a Judean world drastically remade by four centuries of inter-testamental history. It is to Judea and its religious inclinations and difficulties to which our narrative now turns.

CHAPTER TWELVE – DESCENT INTO DIVISION

By 27 B.C. the small nation of incredible and lasting importance could relax and inhale the rarified air of peace. Yes, the Romans were still present but no longer were their great armies tramping across the countryside and laying siege to Jerusalem and other locales. The Pax Romana brought to Rome by Augustus was to be likewise enjoyed in Judea, at least for a while. No civil armies prepared for war against their fellow Jews, but that does not necessarily equate to all matters being tranquil among the Jews. Most certainly, the average Jew resented the unwelcome Roman conquerors, and rightly so. They knew that in the final reckoning their land was ruled by a foreign sword. Tremendous clashes, even wars, remained to be fought with the Romans. Yet for now any overt violence was confined to incidents and what today perhaps be termed gang activity. Too much disproportionality of power existed between Rome and Judea for the Jews to own any chance of casting off their yokes of submission. For certain, many, though not all Jews, did come to hate the Romans, but for them it was a learned experience. Jews despising and loathing other Jews was not learned but rather seemed to be endemic to the group. While this was a time of political pacification the religious and sectarian divisions, with an emotionally violent intensity seemed to come to the fore, and the times promised more of the same. Something was always brewing in much of the populace, and the spirit of many was captured by history's greatest poet, William Shakespeare, some sixteen hundred years later in his immortal tragedy of "Macbeth," wherein the witches chant:

> "Double, double toil and trouble;
> Fire burn and cauldron bubble."

Trouble was always brewing within the Jewish community in the late first century B.C., and always with the specter looming of even more.

The Jews of this time were performing in a somewhat different arena than was typical for their Old Testament ancestors. Much of the old ways which had plagued the children of Israel since the time of Abraham had vanished. Foremost among these was idolatry, which had destroyed the northern kingdom and came within a hair's breadth of ending Judah. The Jews were weaker than before, fewer than ever, yet by the time of their return from exile idolatry had been abandoned. They once had been a nation characterized by a passion to be like other nations, and consequently they had often assimilated the mores and immorality of other nations. Among the Jews a pride had begun to develop, a pride in being separate and apart and a pride in just being a Jew, one of God's special nations, a member of the chosen people. This feeling of pride, distinctness and an ancient form of patriotism is quite informative of the nature of many groups and sects to which the Jews began to divide themselves. They began to illustrate with their lives, their teachings, and their intense "Jewishness" that there exists such a quality as too much or even perhaps, misplaced pride and patriotism. The intensely "religious" Jews, especially those with education, began to divide themselves into sects marked by an increasingly bitter rancor, one with another. This trend, which began to intensify and accelerate following the Maccabean period in the mid-100's B.C., was as intense as ever in the generation before the New Testament.

No one can fully grasp many of the occurrences of the New Testament, especially the four gospels, without understanding the substance and perhaps even the history of several sects who played such prominent roles. Briefly, our narrative will examine these groups, or more accurately the most prominent among them, with a cognizance that many smaller sects, of whom we know less, existed. At the onset of this brief study, it is important to note that this is a review of minorities. The average Jew was not a member of any sect, and those that were comprised a very small minority. It was, though, a minority with an outsized influence, pride, and the ability to make trouble and noise. To proceed with the Shakesperean metaphor at this moment Judea was bereft of wars, though not of an occupying army. The idea of a successful Judean armed rebellion was ludicrous, such was the power differential between Rome and Judea. Still, Judea was a witches' cauldron of dissent, rebellion of spirit if not of arms, hatred for the Romans, hatred, jealousy and resentment of fellow countrymen and an intense desire, so intense that it forever befuddled the Romans, to serve God. There was the rub. The Jewish religion, its leaders and its committed men and women had divided into groups, each with an amazing self-assuredness of the full native of a God whom they had never seen and that God's will about life even to the extent of possessing an adamancy of certainty when God had not spoken. Though Judea boasted many sects we shall briefly discuss four that held a special importance and influence, commencing with perhaps the smallest of the quartet.

THE ESSENES

It is likely that the Essenes were the fewest in numbers of all Jewish sects and most certainly it may be averred that they were the most stringent in their views of their own faith. The historian Josephus estimates that there existed as most four thousand of these basically monastic religious enthusiasts. Today they are renown for a certain monastic bent and their continual scholarship. Just becoming an Essene was quite onerous, which included one year as a postulant followed by another two years of restricted participation in the Essene community. Although the terminology is modern the concepts are ancient in that a new Essene became in economic terms a socialist or even communist when he joined the sect. All, except the bare substances necessary for daily subsistence were surrendered to the Essene community as a whole. Of course, this would include lands, homes, money, and all personal property. The new Essene would work in the fields as a farmer or in various handcrafts under the strictest moral guidelines. It is easy to view the Essenes as the progenitors for many Christian orders which would follow in the coming centuries.

The Essenes were an all-volunteer force whose regimented order and lifestyle would be the envy of the harshest and strictest of any military groups which might follow. They were divided into four ranks and would do nothing unless so ordered by a superior. On a typical day each member rose early, worked at his assigned job until eleven in the morning and then attended the community assembly. All would then dress in loincloths, bathe in cold water and dine on a sparse meal of a piece of bread and one bowl of food. The ate quietly and spoke only when necessary and then only if they had judged to be sufficiently pure and of an unstained character. Somehow, this was to be considered an offering and a glorification of God, although the God of the Old Testament, much less the New, had never required any of this.

The Essenes, to their general credit though, appear to have been sincere, and hypocrisy cannot really be considered a companion of their religion. Known for their spare lifestyle it should not be surprising that their religious beliefs and practices were likewise aligned with a certain simplicity of purpose. Actually, as Josephus records, the Essenes' beliefs had little to do with philosophy but were more concerned with practical morals and ethics. Their teachings placed emphasis on purity and mercy towards others, traits that would be honored by a later Christian writer who remarked that:

> "Pure religion and undefiled before God and the Father is this,
> To visit the fatherless and widows in their affliction,
> and to keep himself unspotted from the world."

The Essenes believed in the immortality of the soul, but Josephus believed that they denied the resurrection. Their teachings on marriage and the family are sketchy, but the Essenes's practical lives bespoke that they held little regard for the world's oldest institution. Nonetheless some retrospective credit is due the Essenes. While it would be improper to state that they foreshadowed Christian teachings (God performed adequate foreshadowing of that Himself), it would b more firmly placed to say that the Essenes understood the essence of much Christian morality. They had a grasp upon the concepts of separateness and withdrawal from the world, foundational Christian doctrines, but their actual practice of withdrawal was wrong. God has never commanded or wanted His children to live hidden from a view of the world. As His Son said we are to be "...in the world but not of the world." The Essenes's literal withdrawal was a result of misguided interpretations. The Essenes's adoption of God's ways was unnecessarily distorted, but their spirit retains a strange inducement to our admiration. Also, the Essenes truly were religious, and they eschewed the increasingly violent maelstrom of contemporary Roman and Jewish politics. The same cannot be said for the next group to whom we direct out study.

THE SADDUCEES

The Sadducees were a political party draped in the holiest robes of religion and masquerading as the wise, prudent men of Judea. As with the Essenes the first historical mention of the Sadducees comes from Josephus who spoke of them as being extant at the times of Jonathan Maccabeus, the last Maccabean leader of the revolt against the Seleucids in 160 to 143 B.C. This fits well historically with the timeline of both the Maccabees and the Hasmoneans, the name by which the Maccabees became known. The Hasmoneans retained a grip on the High Priesthood, and more than any one element the Sadducees became associated, almost synonymous, with the office of High Priest. It was a marriage of both power and subservience to the Romans which, with the exception of a brief interlude or two, remained solid until the destruction of Jerusalem in 70 A.D. The Sadducean High Priesthood became the conduit through which Rome ruled Judea, and both parties were keenly aware of this actuality. Certainly, the Romans had their own officials, most notably their governors, kings, tetrarchs, etc., but it was through the Sadducees that the intersection of Roman and Jew was most pronounced. On the whole the Sadducees performed their self-anointed mission quite well, and later with the consent of the Romans they won their supposedly greatest victory in the Sadducean led conspiracy that killed God's own Messiah.

This has been a truncated summary of the outward nature and most noteworthy duty and accomplishments of this sect, but still, we must examine their character and initially the question of their origin. We will pass upon the complicated and somewhat disputed genesis of the name "Sadducee" and commence with a likely origin story from the Maccabean era. As the narrative has so informed the Maccabees and the Hasmoneans became one and the same. Naturally, with their victory over the Seleucids in the Maccabean Revolt the Hasmoneans claimed not just the laurels but also the spoils of victory. With the priesthood firmly in their grasp quite naturally with the passage of time the High Priesthood and the offices it controlled became somewhat of a very pleasant but private preserve for the Pharisees. Just as naturally time and extended service and power brought prestige, even more power and when necessary, accruing wealth to the Sadducees. It was not shocking that the Sadducees were drawn from what in modern sociological terminology would be the upper and upper middle classes. For the most part, and as the New Testament will bear witness, they became increasingly comfortable in their stations in life.

The great and lasting irony of the Sadducees is that to the present they remain identified as one of the two great religious sects in early New Testament Judaism when they were actually not all that religious. As will be noted they denied much of the great underpinnings and authority of their own religion, a religious community which they claimed to represent well and to lead. So, what form did this denial assume?

The New Testament gospels are informative of one of the basic tenets of the Sadducees, and that is the rejection of the resurrection of the dead. A lack of belief in the next life means so much, but in a discussion of the Sadducees's role in religion it effectively meant that they were representing and exalting a dead or at least a dying religion and its God. Religion is then (or now for that matter) reduced to a sketchy moral template for life, the best way to "get along" and even to prosper. Whether its adherents so realize it is a self-proclaiming doctrine that its religion has no past or future meaning, no promise of anything more than the resent sensory perception of life. The Sadducees effectively preached and taught death, and well they should. They effectively served and worshipped a god of the dead.

As for the moral code which is at the heart of any religion their acceptance of traditional Judaism was quite limited. Only the Torah, the first five books of the Old Testament, did the Sadducees fully accept. That left thirty-four volumes, which included such as the conquest of

Canaan, the judges and kings, uprisings, rebellions, captivities, liberations and prophecy, the Divinity of which they neither accepted nor taught.

The Sadducean moral teachings centered more on their consideration of ordinary virtues, rights, and wrongs and not upon the overriding providence of God. While Christianity itself is exemplified by the teaching of every day moral and ethical guides, but Divinely founded. All in all, the ancient Sadducees in practice and belief seemed to bear a striking resemblance to several modern, nay ultra-modern, mainline Protestant denominations, more concerned with being in the forefront of cultural and religious trendiness and cultural acceptability. The simple truth of the Sadducees is that for all their pomposity, religiosity and holy pretense, real religion was not really a part of their character, as this fact was to be harshly and fiercely demonstrated in the early first century A.D. They were the very embodiment of the people who Paul later excoriated as "...having a form of religion but denying the power thereof." Paul's statement, though, was relatively mild compared to what they heard earlier from the man defined as the greatest of all prophets.

John the Baptist had a way with words, certainly not to the degree of his still more famous cousin whom he preceded, but he grasped the attention of the listener. Early in his ministry, while he was preaching at the Jordan River, he espied many of the Sadducees come to hear him, whereupon he greeted them:

"O generation of vipers, who hath warned you to flee from the wrath to come?"

He challenged them that if they were to become suddenly righteous and religious that they "... Bring forth the fruits meet for repentance." Intellectual and spiritual curiosity would not suffice, and neither would their esteemed Jewish aristocratic pedigree meet the challenge:

> "Think not to say within yourselves,
> We have Abraham to our father;
> for I say unto you,
> that God is able of these stones
> to raise up children unto Abraham."

Never had this self-appointed aristocracy been so chastised, but it was not foreseen by them that another would soon appear who would strip from them forever their venal airs of hypocrisy. How they would hate Him!

John preached an attention getting message, which when coupled with the peculiarities and dynamic personality of the speaker was mesmerizing. In these few words just quoted he struck a two-note chord which was so applicable to the Sadducees yet contained for them no harmonious melody. The first is the reliance upon your ancestry, your parents, your heritage, and your bloodlines is a fool's mission and soul destructive. With their fellow sectarians, the Pharisees, no Jews relied upon their own Jewishness and assumed religioniosity and righteousness more than did the Sadducees. Further, they could add to it the "glamorous," yes to them glamorous, sheen of being the holders and keepers of the priesthood. It was their claimed ancestry and lineage to the great Maccabean family that gave them an added luster and sparkle, or at least so they thought, to everything they did. The Sadducees were the self-assured and self-appointed bluebloods and aristocracy of the Jewish nation, and they demanded a wide berth of recognition and obeisance to the assumed quality. Then this Galilean rustic, this wild man John the Baptist, calls them literally a bunch of poisonous snakes.

The four gospel writers are consistent in reflecting that the three-year ministry of Christ did not detail an extensive amount of dialogue with the Sadducees, and certainly this is consistent with their nature and character. One incident bears discussion, though, since it is so revealing of both Saducean character and doctrine. With noticeable unctuousness the Sadducees approached Christ with a question which was designed to both advance their fundamental tenet of no resurrection and to entrap the Master. What if, they posed, a man took a wife but he soon died, with his brother then marrying her, and the same sequence of events following five times in succession, with a total of seven brothers being married to this one wife, with the woman herself finally succumbing to death. The question was:

> "In the resurrection therefore,
> when they shall rise,
> whose wife shall she be of them?
> For the seven had her to wife?"

The modern term for this is "Gotcha!" The Sadducees believed in no afterlife, and this question was designed to expose the folly of belief in resurrection and to utterly humiliate Christ. On its face, though, it demonstrated the lengths to which the Sadducees would go to make a point. The odds of a single woman marrying seven brothers and having them all die in succession is astronomical. While it was meant for entrapment of a perceived enemy more plainly it revealed the lengths to which the Sadducees would go to demonstrate the presumed truth of their foundational doctrine of no life after death. In the event it showcased the unwavering ability of the Master to evade their entrapment and to elevate the argument and discussion beyond their wizened ability to reason:

> "Do ye not therefore err...

> For when they shall rise from the dead,
> they neither marry, nor are given in marriage;
> but are as the angels which are in heaven."

As beautiful and fulfilling as is the earthly institution of marriage, God's design for His disciples will be far greater in Heaven. The Sadducees were defeated, perhaps even embarrassed, but even then, they sensed that the "final" victory over the upstart Galilean would be theirs. Time and events would provide the answer.

THE PHARISEES

Through the prism of history certain opposing duos, have become inextricably linked together, not really in spite of but because their opposition was so intense that it is hard to imagine one without the other. They may be individuals, parties or even nations and the recitation of one name seems to beg the other to follow. Athens and Sparta, David and Goliath, Napoleon and Wellington, Lee and Grant, Republican and Democrat ad infinitum. One begets the other, and their very open opposition to the other enhances their duality. For the Biblically literate, Sadducee can hardly be uttered without following with the word Pharisee.

The actual origin of the Pharisees is a question of longstanding scholastic dispute and is an arena in which our thoughts are not required to venture. For practical purposes they began to achieve prominence after the Maccabean revolt, and by the time of the Roman's coming in the 60's B.C., they were a major force in Jewish religion and politics, and they continued in that role until the destruction of Jerusalem in 70 A.D. As an earlier chapter reflected the Pharisees and Sadducees were more than academic foes who engaged only in the repartee' of words. They had been engaged in a gruesome civil war when the Romans arrived, these western conquerors eventually aiding the Sadducees, thus relegating the Pharisees to primarily religious and cultural influence. Yet in these two realms the Pharisaical influence was enormous, as even a passing familiarity with the New Testament, especially the gospels, will proclaim. Far more than the Sadducees did the Pharisees partake of ordinary Jewish life although always on their rigidly self-defined terms. Much more than any other sectarians did the Pharisees mix with people, walk with Christ, and ask of Him questions.

Sometimes words, phrases and titles can mask the true character of an individual or organization, but in other instances they may be quiet illuminating. For the Pharisees the latter is certainly more appropriate. The word Pharisee ultimately is derived from ancient Greek and is meant to denote "set apart" or "separated," and for both good and bad the ancient Pharisees of Judea lived up to the literal definition of their title. Properly understood and followed "separateness" is a virtue to a follower of Christ, and in both intellectual and lifestyle terms it is not just a virtue, but a necessity. This is a Divine concept which extends deeply into the Old Testament, and its early exemplars were men such as Noah and Abram, who were called forth by God to come forth and live differently than others. God Himself through His great prophet Moses led he Hebrew people from four centuries of Egyptian slavery, wherein their lives were in bondage and their spirits in pagan shackles. Much of the Old Testament is a millennia long story of the ebb and flow of the Jewish nation and people, wherein is found the disclosure of their desire, often expressed openly and rebelliously, to be like everybody else. Their history, among other things, was a resentment of having to follow laws, traditions, mores, and customs different from the heathen nations which surrounded and often enslaved them. Finally, though, the Babylonian/Persian captivity seemed to shake the Jews from a spiritual lethargy. In the 400's B.C. when the remnant returned to Judah it represented a remnant of a changed people. No more would the Chosen ever succumb to the allures of paganism. The

Israelites continued to have their problems and pitfalls, but the paganistic road had been blocked. They began to develop an awareness and even a pride in being Jews. Then came in the second century B.C. the avaricious tyrant Antiochus Epiphanes IV, a man who unleased upon the Jews a pre-modern version of the Holocaust. Our story has already included the Maccabean Revolt, the marvelously successful uprising of the Chosen, a people who now began to show pride and full self-awareness that as Jews they were different than the Gentile world was always a threat to swallow them whole.

Although no expression is found in either of the Testaments nor apparently in any secular source seemingly an unspoken emotion had descended upon the Jewish people, a feeling of "Never again." Never again would we descend into heathen idolatry and never again would we be ashamed of being Jews. Rightly they believed that God had called them forth and made them separate and apart from the Gentile world. Correctly they began to regard the Law as not a burden, but rather as something precious that marked their uniqueness. In the simplest terms these descendants of Abraham became proud to be Jews. They had pledged themselves to a worthy, noble, and true cause, and no group more than the Pharisees, the strictest of all the multitude of Jewish sects.

In many easily discernible ways, the Pharisees were different from their antagonists, the Sadducees. Whereas the latter was concentrated in the priesthood and upper classes the Pharisees continually touted their representation of the ordinary, common citizens. As with all such generalities reality often impinges upon many individual cases, blurring our efforts at clear cut discernment. It was in their beliefs, though, that the Pharisees truly capture the attention of the student. The Pharisees literally took God at His word and the entirety of the Old Testament, not just the five books of the Torah, they accepted as Divine direction. Wonderful and admirable, yet as with so many good ideas and manners the Pharisees gradually began to go astray.

To the Pharisees the sanctity of the Old Testament eventually became insufficient to direct theirs or any other Jew's life. By the time of Christ in the first century they had added to the Law of Moses what came to be known as the "Oral Tradition," which in the interpretative minds of the Pharisees became unchallengeable. It was this that was condemned by the Master who upbraided them for teaching as truth the "commandments and traditions of men." As one may begin to suspect the oral Tradition became and meant what the Pharisees decreed that it signified. Effectively, the Pharisees, whatever their origins and/or their intentions, presumably good, placed themselves in a sort of earthbound judgment seat where the law was exactly what the Pharisees said it was. In the teachings, conduct and most dangerously in the hearts of the Pharisees this dangerous quality began to solidify. Through the generations in their front ranks were found men such as Hillel, Gamaliel and Saul of Tarsus, men of incomparable mental acuity and breadth of knowledge, all of which were mortgaged to the intellectual elite. In short, for all their original good intentions, which were highly laudable the Pharisees truly became "separate and apart" from others. In short hard terms, they absolutely knew that they were right ... and moral.

Of their beliefs, though not the practice of most, we should remain admiring of the Pharisees. Unlike the Sadducees, an elite priestly upper-class cultlike group the Pharisees proclaimed their openness to all, including the common people. They (at least in theory) spoke of the majesty of God and in direct opposition to the Sadducees proclaimed the resurrection and a new life in Heaven. Their teachings emphasized virtuous moral conduct, but perhaps it is here at the intersection of teaching and actual living conduct that the good in Phariseism began to crumble and dissolve. It was here, too, that the enmity and enflamed hatred of the Pharisees for the Son of God burned brightest. Christ exposed them for what they actually were, hypocrites. He did this not with a single word or phrase but with three years of consistent teaching. Jesus saw their religion to be show and so stated. In a famous parable he contrasted two strikingly different men:

> "Two men went up into the temple to pray;
> the one a Pharisee, and the other a publican.
>
> The Pharisee stood and prayed thus with himself,
> God, I thank thee, that I am not as other men are,
> extortioners, unjust, adulterers, or even as this publican.
>
> And the publican, standing afar off,
> would not lift up so much as his eyes unto heaven,
> but smote upon his breast, saying,
> God be merciful to me a sinner."

It is a certainty that Jesus of Nazareth took no pleasure, no sense of smug satisfaction, in revealing to the world the falsity and arrogance of the Pharisees. We should be reminded of their days, for like many movements and causes they begin with noble intentions that eventually fall prey to the corruption of the world. The ancient Jewish Pharisees were as pure an example of such as may be found. They arose from the ashes of literally centuries of national apostasy, paganism and in the Biblical phraseology of "... whoring after false gods." They had recognized what the Jewish nation had done to itself, first by literally succumbing to the destruction and disintegration of its north and then watching Judah in the south being reduced to a severely truncated few, the remnant which could still serve God's purposes. "Never again" seemed to be the watchword, the battle cry of the early Pharisees. No more would our nation abandon God, ignore His Law and assume the identity of the surrounding Gentiles. We would draw apart, separate from Gentile influences and be strict in our observance of Revealed Truth. Wonderful were their intentions and the lives of many Pharisees (one thinks of Saul of Tarsus) possessed an unfettered spirituality and even a moral admiralty. How, then, did the Pharisees go from this to the reputation of moral squinting, hubris, self-righteous, preening, and moral overbearing which adheres to them two thousand years later? Or, as He always was capable of expressing in the greatest of clarity to that point where Christ declared:

"That except your righteousness shall exceed the righteousness of the scribes and Pharisees,
ye shall in no case enter into the kingdom of Heaven."

A complete fulness of answer to the question remains will God alone, but history, scripture and especially Christ give us a framework, even a superstructure, of an answer.

Doubtless in general (and we speak in generalities) the Pharisees's original intentions were noble and their righteousness genuine. Still, precisely as it yet remains, the temptation, usually unnoticed and silent, for a righteous person to become "self" righteous is ever extant. The Pharisees then, as Christians later and to the present, easily can perceive the world in which they live and begin to feel good about themselves. They survey their worldly surroundings and can easily, even correctly, conclude, that they are better than the world. This belief, though, is the starting gate for all manner of pride and sin. Quickly it leads its practitioner from genuine morality to moral smugness and ultimately to the dais where stood the Pharisee in the Temple proclaiming to God his gratitude that he is better than other men. The Pharisee truly sets himself "separate and apart" from all other men and women save for those who think and act exactly as he does, i.e., other Pharisees. The Pharisee descends to the point where his moral influence wanes to nothingness, or perhaps even worse, to oppressiveness. To a true Pharisee, as the term has become understood historically and morally, only his and the opinions of other like-minded

Pharisees have any validity. His influence for good dies, but his influence for "... all manner of evil remains hale and hearty."

The Pharisees of the late first century B.C. remained influential, and their influence for suppression, destruction and outright hatred remained strong. They were in a manner of speaking "separate and apart" from others, but not to such an extent that they could not subordinate themselves momentarily for the greater "good" of the destruction of a perceived enemy. These separatists and civil warriors could join others for their own causes, and one of the "others" had become as prominent as the Pharisees.

THE SCRIBES

In the strictest sense the scribes were not really a religious sect. The Jews, a highly literate people, had always scribes, who were professional transcribers of all types of documents, from legal documents to any instrument required by the Law of Moses. After the return from exile in circa 400 B.C. gradually they began to assume the duties as interpreters of the Law, and to many Jews they became quite authoritative and respected in this role. They seemingly had no sort of religious organization and appeared to function as a sort of professional guild. Although some scribes were Sadducees it appears that the scribes were more in the nature of an ally, or almost a partner of the Pharisees. No man coupled them together more than Christ and His life and teachings are replete with the phrase "scribes and Pharisees." Although this is not meant to be dismissive of the intellectual prowess of the Pharisees the scribes seemed to function practically as the Pharisees's brain trust and intellectual firepower. Whenever the term "lawyer", rarely to the present a compliment is employed scripturally, it is almost always in reference to a scribe.

The scribes were serious men, and in the literal sense they seemed to follow Jesus with as much diligence and discipline as did His own disciples. As lawyers are endemic inquisitors, they delighted in asking Jesus questions and engaging in a protracted legal and religious debate with the Savior. Generally, their questions revealed great knowledge, and though many were designed to entrap Christ, the inquiries represented the products of finely developed minds.

The scribes were respected in Jewish society, and obviously enjoyed the adulation of others and the praises of being deemed smart and learned. The truth was that they were learned and important, but like so many intellectuals and academics then and now, they came to develop an inflated opinion on their own doctrine and looked with scorn upon those lesser types who had not the presumed education and academic credentials which they so proudly possessed. Although they would have recoiled in horror at such an appellation the scribes and the Pharisees were tribalists, trusting only in like-minded members of their own group. No where was this more plainly and disgustingly shown than when the apostle John recorded their reaction to the officers and soldiers who uttered of Jesus that still attention arresting phrase:

"Never man spake like this man"

The "in" group could abide not only the Galilean upstart but those who were taken in by Him. Then answered the enemies of Christ:

"Have any of the Pharisees or of the rulers believed in Him?"

Only a member of the self-anointed religious orthodoxy could have a belief worthy of respect. If we do not believe Him, said the Pharisees and scribes, then the matter is settled, and the case is closed. We permit the narrative a momentary tangential path to reflect on how similar this was to the oppressively stultifying thinking and opinions of the modern media, newspapers, television, social media, the academy, and the peculiarly modern phenomenon which they essentially created, the celebrity culture. The same beliefs, opinions, doctrines, ad infinitum are with, but a few exceptions shared by all. So, it was with the scribes and their allies, the Pharisees.

All these sects, these groupings of generally intelligent and learned men sincerely held differing beliefs on their construction and interpretation of the Law of Moses and the best, even the ideal path, which the Jewish nation should follow. With such diversity of opinion, often not merely fiercely but ferociously and steadfastly held by so many diverse groups it would have been impossible to find a "peaceful" Jewish society at the end of the first century B.C. This essay has reviewed only the most prominent of Jewish sects, and for the sake of brevity others such as the Herodians and Zealots are only now mentioned.

If all these sectarians had been interrogated it is overwhelmingly likely that they would have asserted that each man desired unity and harmony among the Jewish people, a small populace with a unique history of unity only for relatively brief moments of time. As the first century B.C. could see its end in sight they labored under a unity of sorts, an efficient, harsh when necessary, but always foreign, just as their masters, the Romans, were alien. Religious and moral unity, not always synonymous, seemed to be farther from their grasp than ever. This sort of unity appears capable of growth and flourishing in only two circumstances. The first is the unity of opposition to a common enemy, which they had in Rome. Here, too though, the unity was far from complete because each group had its own well-defined relationship with the powerful conquerors from the west. The two most diametrically opposed but also the two most prominent, the Sadducees ad Pharisees, were radically different in their approaches to the great Empire. The Pharisees eschewed the Romans as unclean Gentiles, while most of the Sadducees had made their peace with them, dependent as they were upon the Romans for the power which they exercised.

In a strange, truly unique manner of the other source of unity the various Jewish sects and denominations would temporarily avail themselves. In so doing they combined this one unifying force with the earlier mentioned element of opposition. So opposed did they become to the purveyor of real unity, Jewish and Gentile, and so bitter and morally profane did their conduct become that the apostle Matthew recorded His evaluation of them with the most devastating excoriation of their conduct and character when repeatedly he indicted them in detail with each bill of particular beginning with the phrase:

"Woe unto you, scribes and Pharisees, hypocrites!"

The substance of their consciences and of their hearts had hardened and congealed the spirit and soul into a unity of opposition. How much better for them and for all of it had been a unity of reference and worship for Him?

For the moment, though, our inter-Testamental study has drawn to its ending. The metaphorically tiny vessel of earlier chapters has reached port, and recognized or not, the Person that it bears will become the most important factor in the life of every man or woman who has ever drawn breath on this earth. At last. His day is at hand.

CHAPTER THIRTEEN - EPIPHANY

Let us be reminded that one Gaius Octavius was the tender age of nineteen when his great uncle Julius Caesar was murdered in 44 B.C. Almost immediately he had proven that he possessed more than just a great and famous name, and by 31 B.C. his enemies Antony and Cleopatra were routed at Actium, and soon they would be dead. For the first time in literally decades, even generations, power in Rome was not up for grabs, as it now rested securely in the youthful, but mature, grasp of Octavian. This man was different than most rulers, though, whether of antiquity, ancient Rome alone or in the entirety of the world's history. He was quite circumspect in his usage of power, and nothing of the self-aggrandizing showboat clung to him. Slowly, carefully, methodically and with an ever-consistent public display of modesty, Octavian consolidated his power.

By 27 B.C. Octavian released both himself and Rome from the dictatorship he had assumed for years as he finally and ostensibly returned power to the Senate, with which in comparison to other consuls, a title which he retained, Octavian maintained a smoother and more cordial relationship. He rejected at first the title of emperor and simply called himself "princeps," or first citizen of Rome. A luminary named Manutius Planus proposed for Octavian the title of Augustus, or "reverend," which he accepted, and hence he becomes known to history as Augustus Caesar, the first emperor of Rome.

From the onset of a reign which was to endure for over forty years, Augustus deliberately cultivated and projected a persona that was the embodiment of traditional Roman values, integrity, devotion to family and to state and a generally solid, even stolid character. With Augustus it was more than a pose. Although he was a jealous guardian of his own power, he became the imperial father to what has become known as either the Golden Age or Augustan Age of Rome. Augustus sought and achieved historical recognition as a man of peace, and his reign did commence the Pax Romana, the Roman Peace, which was sustained for two centuries. For this he is to be commanded, but we must place a check rein on our adulation. Augustus waded through rivers of blood to obtain the throne, and likely would have dealt harshly with any who stood as a potential obstacle. Yet his reign was remarkably peaceful, and both as an emperor and/or man he seemed to actually reach a plateau of satisfaction. During his reign the Roman Empire essentially assumed the shape and boundaries it would maintain for centuries. The Augustan years saw minor growth, but the days of the great campaigns of the likes of Julius Caesar and Pompey the Great were concluded.

Augustus was a builder and later made the famous boast that he had found Rome brick but left it marble. It was not an idle boast, and the public face of Rome began to change, though, the bulk of the increasingly crowded city was a tight pack of cheap, flimsy, wooden housing. Rome was becoming ever more proud of itself, and though various kings, potentates and princes could take an occasional nibble on the Empire's edges, the Roman Empire was unassailable in this, the beginning of its Golden Age. Still, as an observer some seventeen centuries later wisely observed, "... there is a lot of ruin in every country." Rome had its share of ruin, and it would be starkly exposed in the Light that would soon come.

Rome itself, that central Italian metropolis on the Tiber to which all roads led was not growing in isolation. Peace, together with will, money and labor was altering the face of even the most remote stations of Augustus's Empire. In far away Judea a politico extraordinaire, now known as King Herod the Great, reigned over a prosperous land in a prosperous period, and almost simultaneously with Augustus's ascension to emperor Herod began a building program of unparalleled scope. The great king always maintained a vacillating relationship with the Jews, a people he ruled, though Herod himself was less than half-Jewish. His association with the Romans was close, too close for the preferences of many Jews. Too easily and liberally he had himself succumbed to the Gentiles's way of life and a moral philosophy at odds with the Law of Moses. Even more so than most ancient rulers Herod had a penchant for violence and vindictiveness towards anyone whom he could even remotely conceive as a threat. This included multiple political opponents, his own children, and multiple wives, who suffered death at his orders. Still Herod the Great continued to build, including many public buildings, a grand royal palace for himself and most important of all, a rebuilding of the Great Temple in Jerusalem. So magnificent and beautiful it was that Josephus, the historian, was rhapsodic in describing it as a beautiful structure above all others.

Such building on such a grand scale obviously required money, and kings and governments raise money by taxation, increasingly heavy and unpopular under Herod. Still, for much of his reign Herod the Great maintained a very tenuous, though far from dominant, popularity among his Jewish subjects. Herod's area was smaller than that of Rome's emperor, but he was a rival to Augustus as a builder, but even more so than Augustus a builder of structures that would prove shockingly temporary.

As the metaphorical pages continued to drop from the metaphorical calendars the passing of the years, as always, progressed unabated. Both Augustus and Herod found reigns of peace, and to the credit of each, neither seemed to be in any fashion eager to tamper with the serenity their subjects enjoyed. Each continued to build, and doubtless at times their methods were harsh and overbearing, but jobs and constructive work and prosperity were being provided to the populace. At a minimum neither was making war on his own people, and neither Rome nor Judea was in the throes of civil war, a common condition for each nation. Still, no matter the prosperity, the architectural splendor, or the often-beautiful results any discerning observer, then or now, may not allow thoughts to stray from that word "temporary." As rulers these two men, one the ruler of the world's most powerful state and the others the reigning monarch of a small province, were great builders but as a later poet so phrased what they said and built "... was writ in water." Yet, if men of such magnitude and power could establish nothing of real permanence, who, if any, could? Especially in the case of Augustus the resources, money and manpower at his command were practically endless.

It is almost axiomatic that what requires years, even decades, of planning and execution may be destroyed in a matter of minutes, even seconds, even in a practical twinkling of an eye. It is not as recognized or publicized, though, as the distinctions between shock and in noise level between construction and destruction. Here we make reference to three major historical events, each shocking, of varying but enormous consequences, especially to Americans and packing emotional shock and tremors which reverberate yet today. They were acts of deliberate destruction, and for all who were living and sentient at the moment of their occurrence they etched indelible memories into the psyche.

We offer three historical examples. Although it is close to having faded from living memory the date of December 7, 1941, has long been etched deeply into the American memory. All remember where they were and their circumstances when first receiving the news that the Japanese had bombed Pearl Harbor, thus plunging the United States into the murderous cauldron of World Ward II. On Friday afternoon, November 22, 1963, the nation and even the entire world was

DARKNESS BEFORE DAWN | 187

stunned by the news of the assassination of President John F. Kennedy in Dallas. Most recently, and on a date which has given to the world a numerical symbolism, over two thousand persons were instantly slaughtered as two large airplanes, hijacked by terrorists, plunged into the World Trade Center in New York on the forever infamous day of September 11, 2001. These three acts of violence and destruction, spread over sixty years history, and each with its own participating cast nonetheless had a certain commonality. They were sudden, shocking, unnerving, and elemental sense of security which countless multitudes shared. Too, they were highly publicized, the news even in 1941 almost instantly accessible to the majority of the world's population, dominating both the media response and personal conversation for an indefinite period. Or, in the timeworn but tried and true phrase bad news travels fast." But what about good news? Does its velocity match that of bad and does its first dissemination come with the thunderclap jolt and shock of the bad? Perhaps in some cases it does, but let our focus be not on the many, but the one, that one instant when the greatest announcement and proclamation the world will ever hear was made. The event's Advent likely occurred within the period 4-8 B.C., as learned historians, scholars and theologians still debate the exactness of the moment.

No debate should enfold, though, for the location of the event. The great cities of modernity, New York, London, Paris, Washington, Tokyo ad infinitum had not yet been borne. The extant great metropolitan areas of such as Rome, Athens, Alexandria, and Jerusalem were passed over for this event. Instead, it would occur, perhaps even at night, in little but despised Nazareth, the contemptible little Galilean village in the proverbial middle of nowhere. Its original participating cast was but two, one not even a resident of our planet, and the second an unknown teenage girl from this same Nazareth. In the month of June, Gabriel, an angel of God came to lowly Nazareth to meet with this girl, with simple eloquence identified by the great gospel writer Luke as:

> "... a virgin espoused to a man whose name was Joseph,
> of the house of David,
> and the virgin's name was Mary."

In one plain yet beautiful sentence the reader learns that the great Old Testament prophecies of centuries are on the eve of fulfillment. It was as simple and quiet as that, but Gabriel announced to Mary its meaning to her in words still daily proclaimed:

> "And the angel came in unto her,
> and said, Hail, thou art highly favored, the Lord is with thee:
> blessed art thou among women."

Without question anyone reading these words knows the beautiful and magnificent peroration of Gabriel's message:

> "And behold, thou shalt conceive in thy womb,
> and bring forth a Son, and shall call His name Jesus."

With the pure simplicity that is always attendant to the manifestation of Divine Power, the greatest news which humanity would ever hear had been proclaimed, quietly, obscurely, without commotion and without crowds. The shock which it produced in Mary and still produced in all open hearts is the shock, the surprise, not of fear and dread, but of pure joy.

This is not the juncture for contrasts to be drawn between the world and God, for the story of this book has already painted that picture. The world, whether Persian, Greek, Macedonian, Seleucid, Roman or even Jewish is a noisy clamorous cacophony, a bedlam of men and nations striving for power, dominance, and prominence among their fellows and in history itself. It is a noisy den of contest, an arena of battle, whether armed or unarmed, and of men striving, almost salivating, for the glittering crown and prize of power. The winners are exultant, delirious, even drunken with the tonic and elixir which is power and fame, while the losers vanish into the darkness and obscurity of the forgotten.

What were the powerful doing on that June day when Gabriel appeared to young Mary? Since we know not the exact date our question requires speculation, but it is an "educated" specification based upon precedent. Perhaps in Jerusalem the Great Council, the Sanhedrin, was in session. This solemn contingent of seventy astute and learned men was the supreme judicial body of the Jews, its meeting a forum where accused criminal defendants appeared and were tried and where great questions of the Law, which the Jews had in abundance, were debated, and hopefully settled. In Athens, Greece, likely in the Areopagus that contingent of scholars, intellectuals, and pseudo-intellectuals, which so sets even today the image of ancient Greece likely was debating (as so marvelously defined two generations later by the gospel writer Luke), the "next new thing," almost always without conclusion or even consensus. In Rome itself perhaps the storied Senate itself was in session. This impressive body of blue-blooded aristocratic patricians had for centuries ruled Rome. Now, though, the Emperor had clipped its wings somewhat, and it was beginning a long period of decline. Still, it retained power and esteem, and it was an important group of men who made important decisions. Likely, also in Rome itself, the city, empire, and its emperor Augustus were at the amazing zenith of their powers. Maybe Augustus was meeting with his counselors and advisers that day, but maybe not. In the event he rightfully could be called the most powerful man in the world, and on the whole, he utilized his powers fairly and wisely. We may safely aver that whatever any of those men was doing that day, none had any awareness of the day's most important occurrence, the angel's visitation of a young girl, a "nobody" as so defined by the world, in unknown Nazareth, Galilee.

How else, though, would God have made the announcement of the coming birth of the Savior? The actions of mankind invariably were and are noisy, clanging, and clamorous, and the good and great covet attention upon themselves. In God's manifestation of His Advent, it was rather a brief, private conversation between a young girl and a Heavenly agent. For the moment, no one else was even aware. Once more God proved Himself true to His own declaration:

> "For My thoughts are not your thoughts,
> and My ways higher than your ways,
> and My thoughts are not your thoughts."

Let us briefly indulge ourselves in the manner in which mankind, particularly we "modernists" of the twenty-first century might have handled the announcement of the imminent birth of the most important person who will ever live. The event would have been preceded by an insufferably long period of advertisement of what was to come. Of course, these were the days (blessedly so) long before another advent, that of modern media in all its ubiquity and its suppression and intended obliteration of logical thought. The advertising and "marketing" of the coming Messiah's birth ranged between minimal and non-existent. In modern terminology (though hardly that of God) the proclamation of the blessed birth did not start at the top and filter its way downward. In terms of earthly prestige and status it started at the bottom and mainly stayed there. Unknown young girls and angelic messengers from God are not the typical opinion makers in any society, be it ancient or modern. Still, the results of the epiphany which Mary experienced that day in Nazareth could not be hidden, and somehow in the absence of humanity's usual efforts the word was spread.

Mary and Joseph, the earthly father, who soon received a similar epiphany that Mary was expecting a child conceived by God Himself, were to be the honored parents. Both knew, but hardly understood, that Mary was to be the bearer of a miraculous birth, of Gad Incarnate. Still, these two lived in the real world of flesh and blood, and while the nature of the birth was yet to be manifest, the fact that Mary, a young unmarried woman, was daily growing with child was plain for all to see. It is likely difficult for young men and women in a liberal progressive society of the twenty-first century to understand or to even contemplate in any mood short of jocularity the strictures of the Jewish moral code, the Law of Moses, which regulated the relationships between the sexes. It was not so difficult, nor does it remain incomprehensible to any living person who came of age before the full impact of the Sexual Revolution of the late 1960's and 1970's. Premarital sex, fornication and adultery were not only wrong but harshly punishable, even to the point of death for adultery under the Law. Here was an unmarried young girl, obviously pregnant, growing more pregnant by the day, and here also was her betrothed Joseph, a Biblically described "just" and "good" man, who knew he was not the father. Rather than humiliate Mary he sought to deal with the matter privately, that is until God intervened and revealed the true story.

As certain as the rising of the morning sun, many in this small village of Nazareth were certain of the "real" story. The thought of a heavenly impregnation of a presumably nobody of a girl such as Mary was both laughable and sacrilegious. Most knew that on the contrary Mary had become with child in the traditional manner and that her betrothed, Joseph, was certainly the father. Daily the evidentiary proof was growing with the baby, and the impatience and disgust of the Nazarenes was keeping pace. It would be best is Mary was not around, for "out of sight, out of mind," is more than altruism, often being a statement of reality. The young Mary, benefiting from the greatest honor God had ever bestowed, was in a quandary. She needed relief from suspicious eyes, wagging tongues and condemning looks, yet where and from whom could she receive the relief? Only God had the answer, and as He does with a remarkable consistency the answer was beautifully appropriate. Early in the pregnancy Mary left Nazareth and journeyed to the hill country of Judea, where lived her much older cousin Elisabeth. This wise lady was in a situation as remarkably akin to Mary's as could be imagined. She, too, was expecting her first child, yet her pregnancy in its manner was as miraculous as Mary's. Elisabeth was well past the age of childbearing, but she and her husband were soon to become the parents of that most important of prophets, John the Baptist. Excitedly and with relief the young Mary came to visit her cousin, the one person whose experiences knit a kinship with Mary. Elisabeth's eternally famous greeting to Mary did not disappoint:

> "Blessed art thou among women,
> and blessed be the fruit of thy womb."

Here, doubtless received understanding, sympathy, praise, and wisdom from Elisabeth, but all such interludes in life are transient. Respite and rest from problems and labors in this life are but temporary, and eventually, now in the latter stages of pregnancy Mary returned not to Nazareth alone. When she arrived home problems, large difficult problems, were aligning themselves and poised to overwhelm her.

Young Mary and her espoused husband Joseph now received a reminder that not even the most humble and obscure are immune from the actions of the high and mighty:

> "And it came to pass in those days,
> that there went out a decree from Caesar Augustus,
> that all the world would be taxed.

And this taxing was first made when Cyrenius was governor of Syria.

And all went to be taxed, everyone into his own city."

As much as any of us may seek, even passionately desire, to live our lives peacefully and far from the clangor and hubbub of the great we are unlikely to be afforded the opportunity. Augustus and his imperial advisors, comfortably ensconced in distant Rome had no concern for its far-flung populace, for unknown village carpenters and their young expectant brides. Their administration needed money and likely an accurate census. Inconvenience, physical hardship, financial loss or any other burden meant nothing to them. To Joseph it meant he had to travel almost one hundred miles to his native town, Bethlehem. Naturally his traveling companion would be Mary, now due. Travel options were few in ancient times, especially for the poor and humble. They were inland, so no water conduit was available, and neither was any public transportation. Walking was the obvious default of travel, yet Mary was about to deliver a baby. For her a one-hundred-mile walk seemed preposterous, and as history and art have generally depicted, it is likely that she rode on a donkey, still a torturously uncomfortable way to travel in her condition. Off they went, though, on a hard, harsh journey, likely the most noted and studied short trek in the world's history. The portent and promise of that which the donkey bore is still staggering in its everlasting effects.

Almost all would have said that Augustus Caesar, First Citizen of Rome and its first emperor, was the most powerful and important man in the world. King Herod of Judea likewise exercised enormous clout, and his moods and dispositions could never be ignored. The Sanhedrin, the Great Council which sat in Jerusalem and debated, counseled, and ruled on the ancient Law of Moses was of great repute and impactful on the daily lives of the Jews. On those days in which Mary and Joseph traveled to Bethlehem, though, none of these great personages were as important as the single donkey which bore young Mary. From this, the most often told story of all history we know that the donkey carried Mary to no mansion or palace, not even to a cheap inn because all were full. Mary and Joseph found themselves in an animal stable, likely with the donkey present, and the young Mary gave birth to the Salvation of the world, and then promptly lay Him in an animal's feeding trough. We have no historical accounts of the births of Augustus Herod, the high priests, and others, but none could have matched this one for simplicity and humility. The child of Mary and Joseph was to provide the answer to the question that concluded the poem "the Second Coming" by the Irish poet William B. Yeats who asked:

> "And what rough beast, its hour come round at last,
> Slouches towards Bethlehem to be born?"

The birth of Mary's baby in that stable was the commencement of the answer to the question of the poet Yeats. Yet it took His whole life, death, burial and resurrection and the still active proclamation of His Word and Character to provide the fullest answer to the poetic question. It was not a "rough" beast that was wanting to be born, but rather Truth itself and the pure manifestation of God. No general, no conqueror with a blood drenched sword and no regally berobed emperor or priest began this new world. Rather, it was God Himself made manifest as a man, the Son of Man, and as Christ, the Son of God. He began, as we all do as a baby conceived (albeit miraculously) in His mother's womb and still provides the Light of the world. The great awe-inspiring persons and institutions which in the world of His birth seemed to tower over humanity have been reduced to pages in history books. No more do the eagles of the Roman empire strike awe and fear into men's hearts, no more does the name Herod mean anything save in an historical sense and no more does the Jewish Sanhedrin convene in Jerusalem. They, so large and imposing, just as were the ships in port, the persons walking along the dock and the hubbub of activity in the long-ago picture described in the Preface no longer exist. As God began His terrestrial creation with "Let there be light" so also did He regenerate that Light when the small vessel on the distant horizon finally came to port. That seemingly insignificant speck on the horizon was the Light of the World.

CHAPTER FOURTEEN – THE PREPARATION OF THE CANVAS

Who knows what God is thinking? So often this question is posed as a type of conundrum which is obviously meant to strongly imply that no man or woman can ever know what the designs of the Almighty are. Often it is a line, which when offered in the negative, is meant to stifle and even quash all discussion on the subject. Theologically, the ultimate destination for the spiritual traveler who accepts that God's thinking is beyond mere mortals will be absolute libertinism and a salacious, avid desire for Satan's first promise that "... ye shall be as gods." Of course, no one has ever known what God is thinking that is unless He has told us or shown us what he is thinking. While it is true that the preponderant enormity of the universe's knowledge is known but to God to, we terrestrial creatures of this world He has been abundantly generous. In addition to the revealed truth of His Word, God has not hidden from our eyes and comprehension an inexhaustibly rich pantheon of His thinking and His goals. The great Psalmist David gave poetic utterance that:

> "The heavens declare the glory of God,
> and the firmament showeth His handiwork.

> Day unto day uttereth speech,
> and night unto night showeth knowledge."

To the believer Revealed Truth is, of course, the Holy Bible, but God's thinking and designs are likewise revealed in His creative glories. Surely most of humanity sees a Divine presence in the various beauties of nature, from, as David said, the firmaments, the rainbows, mountains, landscapes, the innocence of animals and babies ad infinitum. Less often, though, will we acknowledge that in some measure God's design is played out in the affairs of nations and empires, of conquering, yes, even murdering monarchs and generals, even in corrupt religious leaders and maybe even in corrupted religion itself.

Sometimes humanity must have the distance of time, and in large amounts as we measure such, in order to see any sort of plan, much less a "Divine" charter in what soon becomes "history." The plan was present, though, and two thousand years have elapsed since the intertestamental four hundred years. Hopefully, it has been seen that it was one of the richest periods in all history, with political, cultural, military, artistic, legal, and premier of all, religious developments. To the believer it cannot be waved away as a silent period between the Old and the New. Rather, the Hand of God was on all, just as He was with Abraham, Jacob, Joseph, Moses, David, Elijah, the apostles, and the Savior Himself. To aver that God acted in the lives of men such as these is, to a disciple, the proverbial equivalent of pushing against an open door. Something in our moral centers, though, rebel against the concept that likewise God directed His desires through the lives of men of the caliber of Alexander the Great, Julius Caesar, Mark Antony, the Seleucid monster Antiochus IV Epiphanes and Herod the Great. All these evil men played significant parts in God's great Plan of Redemption just as assuredly as did the aforementioned Biblical giants. The Old Testament especially is replete with examples of God's Divinely adept usage of humanity's evil purposes molded by

God to further His greater aims, and the great book is not hesitant in proclamation of such. In ancient Egypt God hardened Pharaoh's heart to such a degree that the greatest nation on earth suffered the equivalent destruction and suffering of total war until Pharaoh saw the identity of the true God in Egypt. Earlier Joseph at the time of the great reconciliation with his brothers explained to them that although they had done great evil to him, their younger brother: Upon their father Jacob's death the older brothers were fearful of the power of the younger brother. They need not have worried, for Joseph assuaged and calmed them with:

> "But as for you,
> you thought evil against me:
> but God meant it unto good,
> to bring to pass,
> as it is this day,
> to save much people alive."

Should our small work need a designated theme sentence the great Joseph so provided it.

The four hundred years between the return of the remnant of the Jews from exile to the appearance of the angel to Mary is an exciting, action-packed drama, one that is Bursting with the names of great civilizations, famous battles, historical giants, both men and women, and of evil run amok. The Lord of Hosts causes no one to sin or stumble, nor does He even tempt any down that path, but His utilization of men and women and their sordid designs and affairs is incessant. He did (and does) use sinners for His purposes, and often they live and die with no knowledge of their being so usage or of God Himself.

It began with as tough and hardened a group of professional soldiers battling for freedom and the infant rising phenomenon known as Western Civilization in a crowded pass in northern Greece known as Thermopylae. These 300 Spartan warriors, raised in a cauldron of overblown masculinity and militarism were pagans to a man, and it was to a man they all died on the sword points of an overwhelming horde of Persian warriors from the east. To a man also they were all pagans who worshipped the countless deities of the Greeks. Yet God utilized these brave men, immortalized in history, to staunch the Persian flood and bestow upon the nascent civilization of Greece time to blossom and flower into the foundation of the West, the main tableaus upon which God would reveal His ongoing plans for man's redemption. As we saw, a rarely unified Greece defeated the Persians, and a culture of such richness and true diversity veritably exploded in a kaleidoscope of color, knowledge, richness and true (not political) diversity such as the world has never seen. Maybe only God could have arranged for this truncated force of warriors to be at an obscure pass for three days as they repulsed the Persian tsunami. Greece thus had time and space to grow and to develop its spirit which led to the phenomenon known as Hellenism, which would go a long distance in undergirding Western thought and society, and in many forms remains, albeit diminished, a force in the modern age. Hellenism was essentially a catchall term for all things and qualities Greek, including that spirit of free inquiry which marked it, the striving for achievement and knowledge, the snobbery and arrogance which became hubristic and a sort of intellectual and even political insularity which so defined ancient Greece.

For all the abundance and glory of their ancient cultural accomplishments, which seemed to crest in the 400's and 300's B.C., a miasma of insularity clung to the Greeks, perhaps even of necessity. The Greeks became ever more proud of their culture and lifestyle and were not the colonizers and empire builders which so marked the Romans in the centuries to follow. The historic assignment of spreading the Hellenistic way of thought and life was not assumed by an Athenian, a Spartan, a Corinthian etc., but rather by an outlier and an interloper who really considered himself more Greek than any of those natives. He was Alexander, King of Macedon, who building upon the work and legacy of his amazing father King Philip II sprinted through the world, humbling ancient states and disseminating the ideas of Hellenism, a common cultural reservoir from which all were urged to partake A Macedonian, considered a rough semi-barbaric people to the north o Greece, Alexander was fully and fanatically committed to two purposes, the spread of Greek civilization and his own almost incomprehensibly gargantuan appetite for fame and power. As the earlier chapters reflect, he has been christened with the title of "God's Great Servant," though it is almost a certainty that he was oblivious to the God of the Scriptures. For the period covered by this study, the inter-testamental era, he must be considered the most significant figure, at least overtly, in God's plans. Alexander remade much of the world, including tiny Judah, and though he shrank no part of the globe the world itself was tightened into closer bonds of which he, perishing at the age of thirty-three, enjoyed little personal benefit. Alexander's talents, skills, and ambitions to both his contemporaries and to many yet today seem almost super-human, but he provided a wonderfully stark example of how God has always employed the strangest specimens for His greater purposes.

Not only can they be strange but also evil in the purest, most unassuaged sense, and Judah under the successors to Alexander was to suffer a firestorm and maelstrom of horror and cruelty the Jewish people would not again experience until the blood soaked ideological firestorm that was the twentieth century The Seleucids, Greco-Syrian successors to a large portion of Alexander's empire, to the inclusion of Judah, in the early second century B.C. spawned a king who took the name Antiochus IV Epiphanes, whose story has briefly been recounted in Chapter Sox. Antiochus desire was an even vaster empire than that which he had already acquired, and ultimately this meant either alliance with or conquest of the great rising power to the west in Europe, Rome. Personally rebuffed and humiliated by the Romans he and his army slinked back home, but his rage was so great that it could be slaked only with the blood of a scapegoat, the Jewish nation and people. Epiphanes basked in a self-perception that he was the new Alexander, a ruler fated not to rule just a desert monarchy but a mighty empire. The Romans with great aplomb had humiliatingly demoted his several rungs on his own self constructed ladder to glory. But such a man would not creep away quietly, as he set to work consolidating and strengthening his own empire to a planned pinnacle of strength sufficient to challenge Rome. His great annoyance remained this strange ethnicity, the Jews, with their preaching and prattling about their Law, their revered prophets, and the weirdness of having one God. Further, alone among the ancient nations whose lands and histories were touched by Hellenism the Jews rejected it, preferring their own ancient culture and one God. Not for the last time did a dark cloud of destruction loom over the Jews. Epiphanes decreed that the Jews would either submit fully to paganism, Hellenism, and any other "ism" which either he or his ruling elite deemed as an imperative, or they would be destroyed. Epiphanes had meant it, for in the 160's B.C. tens of thousands of Jews began to fall to Seleucid swords, suffering grotesque, macabre deaths which threatened the Jews's continuance as a people.

But, really, may the reader legitimately inquire did the God of Creation, the God of Abraham, Isaac and Jaco and the God of Moses have any hand in all this? A man such as Epiphanes can never attain satisfaction for his maniacal ambitions, and so often untold numbers die, destruction becomes their calling card, and they leave a legacy of sadness and hopelessness. The progenitor of such men is not God, but Satan, yet God ultimately bends their evil purposes and lives to His greater plans. Epiphanes was destroying a nation, but his desires collided with one of the most remarkable families in history led by an old patriarch named Mattathias, who had five sons. Together this family achieved a fame that has never diminished, and they are known to us as the Maccabees. As has been recounted this remarkable family led a rebellion against Epiphanes, a rebellion which ousted the tyrant and cost the lives of many Jews, including two of the Maccabean brothers. For Judah, though, it gained independence and even gave a form of unity to a small populace which had a centuries long historical tradition of division, civil war, and internecine fighting. Most importantly the Jews, at last, in large numbers began to "turn religious," eschewing the idols and paganism with which they had plagued themselves. The Law of Moses and humanity's relationship began to be important to many people, and although by their words and actions they were shown to have badly misinterpreted Divine Will, at least their minds; if not their hearts, began to be occupied with matters of the Spirit. Though they were still Jews, the past Epiphanes and post Maccabean generations were not the Jews, still basically pagan of the Egyptian exodus nor were they necessarily the Jews of the period of Kings, judges, and prophets. These descendants of Abraham began to take pride in being Jews, in their history, their traditions and customs and their Law, or in the case of the latter their interpretation of the Law. As the first century A.D. lay on the horizon, at long last the Chosen People, the Jews, had become "religious." A strong element in their natural character remained unshaken from its place of honor. The Jews maintained a running dissension among themselves, now strongly incorporating sectarian religious beliefs. So great was the dissension and the internal wrangling that it became a preeminent factor in the Jews loss of independence, this conquerable Leviathan far away from Judah (now to become Judea) in distant Europe, Rome.

All nations and ethnicities have their histories, and no matter how small or seemingly insular and unaffecting of the larger world history, they do not fade to oblivion. Nonetheless in the last century B.C. the republic of Rome, eventually to become the Empire of Rome, began to dominate both its present and future histories at a level and depth rarely achieved by other nations and civilizations. At first its influence upon the tiny Biblical heartland of Judea seemed to be negligible and before 63 B.C. practically non-existent.

Rome, in the center of the Italian peninsula, had achieved size, power and greatness by absorbing the other Italian lands on that peninsula. Its expansive appetite spread in all directions, and by the time of the last century B.C. it was ready to begin its most aggressive period of conquest. The Romans, though, although their power by then was immensely greater than the tiny Jewish nation had ever assumed, suffered from much the same problem as did the Jews, internal strife, and endless civil wars.

By the commencement of the first century B.C. the Roman colossus had beaten all challengers, including most famously Carthage, led by its uniquely brilliant general Hannibal, in the Punic Wars. Rome had absorbed and consolidated multiple lands and cultures, and it was more than prepared for second and third helpings of a world increasingly within its grasp. It was within the brackets of this century that not only was the Roman Empire born but also it received its shape and size which have characterized it through the millennia of history. Its accomplishment, though, was not through any straight path of historical progression and victory, for the first century B.C. is also the history of Rome at war with itself. The noted and famed personages of its history still loudly ring a bell of recognition with us today. Names of the stature and importance of Marius, Sulla, Pompey, Crassus, Julius Caesar, Brutus, Cassius, Mark Antony, and Octavian still echo with familiarity and fame. Yet all, with the exception of Cleopatra, Egyptian queen but Greek by ethnicity, were Roman, all Gentiles who had likely heard of Judea and its population of Jews but even more likely knew nothing of the strange Jewish tradition of monotheism and the even more puzzling God they worshipped and His law which they followed. Before mid-century, though, the Roman and Jewish worlds had collided. The world of the New Testament which was about to follow

DARKNESS BEFORE DAWN | 205

would be a Roman world, and all its stories, characters, biographies, clashes, and miracles would occur on lands where tribute was owed and paid to the Caesars in Rome.

The men who took the Roman writ and army to Judea were a varied sort, but history rules that not one could be considered a moralist of any sort. They advanced and prospered by the sword, and it was the sword which afforded the conquest of Judea in 63 B.C. Any religion which they possessed was only a pro forma acknowledgement of the panoply of their own gods and goddesses (and in this respect were they really any different than our modern politicians?). Morality meant little to them as their supreme standards of success were the advancement of Roman sovereignty and their own personal political aggrandizement.

For our interests, though, a grand question hovers over all this rapid summation of Roman history. What did any of this have to do and what effects did any of it have on the great Roman figures and contenders for power mentioned earlier is even mentioned in the New Testament, that being Octavian, and even then, it is by his imperial title of Augustus Caesar that he is referenced. The first answer to this question does not need any deep dive into the Divine or spiritual. These were the men, especially Julius Caesar and Pompey who by repeated and brilliant military campaigns "made" the Roman Empire in the first century B.C. Especially, Pompey, who as a conquering hero trampled through the Great Temple, including the sacred Holy of Holies, n 63 B.C. and thereby welded the fates of Rome and Judea together.

The people of Judea were the beneficiaries of the Roman grant of more than a modicum of independence, especially in the spiritual and religious realm, always associated with the Jews but now the very mark of their existence. In point of fact the Jews essentially were given an absolute grant of freedom of religion by the Romans, but only so log as the Jews kept a couple of conditions, which are susceptible to a simple definition of two words, peace and money. The Roman coffers demanded continual replenishment, and the despised collection system of the publicans, most native Jews, kept the treasury full. Perhaps more importantly, though, the Romans insisted upon peace and serenity, and their breach would result in savage retribution by the nighty Roman state.

Although its fame exceeds that of any other it was not Rome alone which made the ancient world or even just the era between the scriptural testaments. Rome, though, was one of three primary civilizations, all of which had met each other by the latter half of the first century B.C. and whose coalescence fashioned the world of the New Testament. Rome, as pagan a state as had ever been known was drawn eastward by a combination of commercial necessity, and the spectacular success of General Pompey provided the opening he and the Roman legions needed for their access into Judea. By a strange mixture of Roman military might, Jewish civil war and political opportunisms by both the Romans and certain Jewish sects' Roman sovereignty was fully established by 63 B.C. When the New Testament's pages began to be filled approximately sixty years later it was a world where every square inch of territory was ruled by the mighty city on the Tiber.

Still, while the Romans were the masters of this world with the vaunted military, their administrative, political, and engineering skills most of the lands had been previously subdued and influenced intellectually, culturally and artistically by the other famous people of the ancient, classical world, the Greeks. The Greeks, both subdued and inspired by the Greek-Macedonian father and son tandem of Philip and Alexander had conquered so many nations, and everywhere their alluring cultural ways and patterns called Hellenism had deeply penetrated into the core of many of the lands Rome now ruled, including and especially Rome. The blood-letting record of the Macedonian duo, especially Alexander the Great, competes well within that of any of history's conquerors. While Alexander was shedding blood, though, he was also disseminating Greek culture, especially including that most precious and widespread of Hellenistic gifts to the world, the Greek language. Although admittedly we are lacking great mountains of statistical data from ancient times (blessedly so) by the first century A.D. the Greek language certainly had become second nature and the second language to much, if not most, of the Empire's population. Most importantly its knowledge did not seem to be confined to a small administrative, academic, or intellectual caste, but was a practical tool for all strata of society. From learned scholars and priests, Roman soldiers, and centurions to Galilean fishermen a plain everyday tongue, "koine" Greek, was spoken. No greater mark of its acceptance throughout society, be it Greek or "barbarian" can be noted than by a recognition that the twenty-seven books of the New Testament were with one authorial exception penned by Jewish writers but in the Greek language. For all this and the spread of the beneficial effects of Greek culture all roads lead back to Alexander the Great. He spent his abbreviated earthly sojourn of thirty-three years drenched in blood, oblivious to the one true God, yet he proved to be a marvelously effective servant of that God. Alexander and his Hellenism carved and paved a road of glory for himself, but the latter disciples and evangelists of God Traveled those roads extensively.

The second of the three great civilizations that coalesced in Judea in the second half of the first century B.C., was of course, the Latin or Roman. They richly deserved their yet extant reputation as harsh and exacting masters, but when their subject peoples thought of them it is doubtful that these were their sole characteristics. When the Jews pondered their fate under Roman rule likely they thought, as do all people, of money and just how expensive Roman rule was proving to be. Rome was a giant foreign government, a gargantuan beast ever hungry for more taxes, more tribute, more of the hard-earned substance of the Jewish nation. These rulers and administrators with their uniformed legionaries from the west could be contemptuous of the Jews, themselves a people who had a high opinion of their own value and place in the world. The Romans were pagans, Gentiles and in continual New Testament vernacular "dogs" to the Jews. They brought with them a different look, different morals, different gods, but the Romans also carried law, stability and to God's purposes, above all, peace. For a century the Romans had conquered others and then slaughtered themselves in seemingly endless civil war. Now with Augustus on the imperial throne, the Pax Romana, the Roman Peace, had begun, and all the empire, including Judea benefited. What's more, with the arrival of the Romans Judea was subject to a force that had the power to "keep the peace." Perhaps it was if God Himself had arranged a temporary truce, an armistice, in the affairs of a world that had bee at war for millennia, and that the Romans were His unknowing agents for maintaining that peace.

To our retrospective gaze the Greeks seemed almost to have invented the ancient world, for to we westerners our study of the ancients invariably begins with the great civilization which they wrought from the soil and rocks of ancient Attica. The richness of what they planted produces a continual harvest of rich knowledge, science, art, and language, all of which are now subjects for scorn in these times of the "woke culture." The glories of Greece were overlaid with the grandeur of Rome, whose civilization and deeds began to blossom somewhat later. After a century of internal bloodletting the Roman state, its leader and likely its very population was exhausted. They were no longer citizens of a republic but now subjects of a mighty empire, spread so far as to encompass remote little Judea. The Romans were the masters, but they came with a cornucopia of gifts that were not diminished by their giving. The Romans brought law, stability, assurance of a secure civil society, and they brought a culture that fostered prosperity. Law and order were more than watchwords to the Roman rule, for they were among its very pillars.

The Roman presence in Judea in those times of the Advent and Life of the Messiah was essential to God's Plan of Redemption. It took the Jewish priesthood, power brokers and sectarians little time before they came to the frightful realization that this man, according to their perverted perception of the Law, was anathema to them. As early as the opening days of His ministry in Capernaum they sought His death for some three years. This lone Galilean might have been easy to dispatch except for the presence of the Romans, who the Jewish establishment was loath to offend. It took them three years before the conspiracy could congeal and His blood shed, three years in which Christ lived under the protective shield of Rome.

As we come to the end of this brief, admittedly incomplete narrative of the four-hundred-year scriptural silence let us now be done with the tales of powerful men and their deeds, often vile but somehow just as often refashioned to God's purposes. We place to the side the swagger of generals, the terror of huge armies and the hubristic self-glorifying which afflicts men and women of all nations and creeds. None knew that each was helping to prepare the path, a true path for the way that God would show from the darkness. The Creator of the Universe had begun with his first words in Genesis:

"Let there be Light."

From the fall in Eden men and women had willingly, apparently with greedy avariciousness dwelled in darkness, as humanity which had been fashioned to live in a bright world lit by God had turned to the morbid grotesque darkness of Satan. The darkness was dispelled that night in Bethlehem, as now God had given the world the purest light of the universe. Only a few then perceived it, as only a few have ever comprehended. That Light, the son of God has His disciples and that apostle closest to Him so expressed this upon the Savior's birth:

> "For the Light shineth in darkness,
> and the darkness comprehended it not."

That Light, neither then nor now, was not Alexander the Great, Julius Caesar, Herod the Great or the great Jewish priesthood and Sanhedrin, none of whom ever saw or comprehended. It was a real Light, and it was of startling suddenness, beauty and intensity seen by some on that long ago night:

> "And there were in the same country
> shepherds abiding in the field,
> keeping watch over their flock by night.
>
> And lo, the angel of the Lord came upon them,
> and the glory of the Lord shone around them..."

To these simple shepherds and to all His disciples the Good Shepherd had arrived, never to leave them. The darkness had been dispelled.

www.ingramcontent.com/pod-product-compliance
Lightning Source LLC
Chambersburg PA
CBHW061036050426
42450CB00028B/988